The Greenspan Commission

THE GREENSPAN COMMISSION
What REALLY Happened

Robert M. Ball

A CENTURY FOUNDATION BOOK

The belief is widespread that the Greenspan Commission, created in 1981 to address Social Security's financing crisis, was a great success. Today, politicians often cite it as a model with which to address complex political challenges. But did the Greenspan Commission really succeed —or did one member find a way to work around its failure? This chapter from Bob Ball's forthcoming memoir explores that question.

The Century Foundation Press • New York

The Century Foundation sponsors and supervises timely analyses of economic policy, foreign affairs, and domestic political issues. Not-for-profit and nonpartisan, it was founded in 1919 and endowed by Edward A. Filene.

LIBRARY OF CONGRESS CATALOGING-IN-PUBLICATION DATA

Ball, Robert M. (Robert Myers), 1914-2008.
   The Greenspan Commission : what really happened / by Robert M. Ball.
   p. cm.
   Includes index.
   ISBN 978-0-87078-517-7
   1. United States. National Commission on Social Security Reform. 2. Social security--United States. 3. Social security--United States--Finance. I. Title.

HD7125.B2786 2010
368.4'300973--dc22

2010010972

PHOTO CREDITS:
The following photos are from the personal collection of Robert M. Ball
Page 9: Greenspan Commission group photo (1982)
Page 55: Claude Pepper at microphones (January 15, 1983)
Page 71: Bob Ball with Tip O'Neill, January, 1983, inscribed by O'Neill

Page 66: President Reagan signing 1983 amendments, Social Security Administration photo collection
Page 33: NCSC protest, Bettmann/CORBIS

Manufactured in the United States of America. Cover design: Claude Goodwin. Interior design: Susan Elliott. Special thanks to Susan Elliott for her assistance in preparing this book.

A Note from The Century Foundation

Over the years, it was our privilege at The Century Foundation to work with Bob Ball on his own publications and to have his advice with regard to our efforts to explain, defend, and advocate social insurance. On these topics, Bob Ball exercised preeminent influence over several generations of public officials and scholars. He understood Social Security and Medicare better than others because he had a major hand in shaping these programs for decades.

In these times when the dysfunction of Congress and the sharp edge of partisanship seem to make any sort of reasonable compromise impossible, this reflection on Ball's experience with the Greenspan Commission is especially timely. We are delighted to publish this volume, which is an excerpt from the forthcoming memoir, *In a Great Cause: My Life with Social Security.*

We thank Tom Bethell for his editorial work, which made this book possible.

RICHARD C. LEONE, *President*
The Century Foundation

Editor's Note

Robert M. Ball (1914–2008) devoted his entire professional life to building and defending Social Security. For more than half a century he was the program's "most influential advocate, architect, and philosopher," in the words of the late Senator Edward M. Kennedy. He went to work at the Social Security Board in January 1939, less than four years after the program was enacted. During the Truman and Eisenhower years, he rose through the ranks of the (renamed) Social Security Administration to become its top civil servant. He then served as commissioner of Social Security under Presidents Kennedy, Johnson, and Nixon, guiding the evolution and expansion of the program; he was also a principal planner of Medicare and its first administrator. After leaving government service he served on numerous advisory councils and commissions, including the National Commission on Social Security Reform, better known as the Greenspan Commission. He also co-founded the National Academy of Social Insurance, wrote many articles and books, and — in his 90s — fought hard and successfully to help defeat President George W. Bush's campaign to begin privatizing Social Security.

Until just days before his death, in January 2008, Bob was working on a memoir of his seven decades of service to the nation. Although the manuscript as a whole was still in draft form and incomplete, he was particularly determined to set the historical record straight with respect to what the Greenspan Commission did and did not accomplish in 1983, and his chapter on the commission is by far the longest and most detailed in his memoir.

I had the great privilege of working with Bob Ball in his later years as his editor and occasional co-author, and I hope to publish his entire memoir. But I feel a special responsibility to help ensure that Bob's chapter on the Greenspan Commission sees the light of day — especially at a time when, once again, there is much talk of a looming "entitlement crisis," and a bipartisan commission has been created to address it, with the Greenspan Commission routinely cited as its successful model. Bob

Ball knew better than anyone the true story of how the genuine Social Security crisis of the 1980s was actually resolved, and his cautionary chapter on the Greenspan Commission should be required reading for policymakers today. I have added an introduction to supply historical context for readers who may not recall the unfolding drama of 1981–83.

— *Thomas N. Bethell*

Contents

The Greenspan Commission:
What *Really* Happened

Editor's Introduction

Ronald Reagan was sworn in as president of the United States at 11:57 A.M. on January 20, 1981. At that moment Social Security faced a highly uncertain future.

For several years the program's financing had been thrown into disarray by the economic turmoil of the 1970s. Revenues, which were primarily dependent upon reasonably robust payrolls, had dropped far below projections as unemployment rose and wage levels stagnated. Outlays, on the other hand, were skyrocketing.

Benefit levels had been linked to inflation since the adoption in 1972 of automatic annual cost-of-living adjustments (COLAs) — a change that seemed to make perfect sense at the time. The adoption of COLAs would not have triggered a financing crisis in prior years, because inflation had rarely exceeded 4 percent per year from 1950 to 1970. But in the mid-1970s inflation became a major problem, and by 1980 it was running at close to 15 percent annually. With outlays for benefits thus outstripping revenues by billions of dollars every year, it quickly became apparent that in the absence of corrective action the system would eventually be unable to pay full benefits on time. When that date arrived, checks due to go out to more than 36 million Social Security beneficiaries would have to be held up, with unimaginable consequences. The dreaded day might arrive as soon as mid-1983 — or even, by some estimates, as early as October 1982, just before the mid-term elections.

The long-term projections made in 1972 had assumed that Social Security would remain solvent far into the future because wages would continue to rise faster than prices. This was an assumption broadly shared among economists, since the pattern had long been a salient characteristic of the U.S. economy and hardly anyone thought that underlying conditions would radically change. But then they did, and practically overnight. The OPEC oil embargo of 1973 was the first in a series of blows to the economy that combined to produce a previously unknown phenomenon that came to be called "stagflation" — a toxic mix of high inflation and high unemployment. According to the conventional economic wisdom, this phenomenon couldn't happen, because it was common knowledge that inflation could occur only if wages were rising rapidly enough to create excess demand for consumer goods. But the unanticipated energy prices of the 1970s, metastasizing throughout the economy and driving up costs so much that manufacturers had to lay off workers and shrink payrolls, did not fit the script. Although energy prices were not the only cause of stagflation, they had an impact powerful enough to overturn the conventional wisdom — and Social Security, through no fault of its own, became trapped in what has been seen in hindsight as a perfect economic storm. Corrective amendments enacted in 1977 proved insufficient to solve the problem.

The result was that by 1981 the program was in serious trouble. The funding crisis could be viewed as temporary, because soon the larger-than-average generation of postwar babyboomers (born from 1946 to 1954) would be reaching their peak earning years, and in the 1990s their payroll taxes would be more than sufficient to pay for the retirement benefits of the smaller-than-average Depression-era generation. But in the midst of the maelstrom the challenge was to chart a course that would bring Social Security through the short-term financial shoals to the safe haven beyond. The program's defenders wanted it to arrive intact. Others saw the crisis as an opportunity to change course.

Ronald Reagan, philosophically opposed to all big government programs other than military, had long been a critic of Social Security, but he had mostly avoided talking about it during his 1980 campaign — with good reason. Four years earlier, running against President Gerald Ford, he had learned the hard way — by losing the Florida primary and thus the Republican nomination — that it was unwise to speak in front of microphones about making Social Security voluntary or otherwise suggesting radical alterations to the program. He was careful not to repeat that mistake while campaigning to unseat President Jimmy Carter in 1980.

Once elected, however, Reagan revisited one of his favorite themes, declaring in his inaugural address that "government is not the solution to our problem; government is the problem." He pledged to downsize the federal government by shrinking its funding across the board. Social Security's finances were, in 1981, still part of the unified federal budget (from which the program would only later be separated). So Social Security was not immune, and trimming it could be seen as consistent with the president's across-the-board pledge. Moreover, while many options were available to improve Social Security's financing for the short term, in one way or another they all required either raising taxes or cutting benefits. Reagan had no intention of raising any taxes for any reason. Indeed, his centerpiece political promise was to cut personal income taxes 30 percent in three years while somehow balancing the budget at the same time. That seemed to make Social Security benefit cuts inevitable.

On the other hand, although Reagan had won the White House, he was not in full command of Capitol Hill. He faced a Democratic majority in the House, and while Republicans nominally controlled the Senate, their enthusiasm for drastic budget-cutting was often more rhetorical than real. Reagan's advisers believed that he could prevail only by being prepared to move as quickly as possible after the inauguration. To make that happen he would need the help of a Capitol Hill insider who was fully committed to his cause and capable of generating complex budget proposals on a tight deadline. That assignment went to David Stockman, who was appointed to head the Office of Management and Budget.

Stockman exceeded even Reagan in the zeal with which he approached the task of transforming government. A 34-year-old two-term Republican congressman from Michigan, he had won re-election in 1980 but resigned to join the incoming administration. His inherent conservatism coupled with his disdain for the workings of Capitol Hill had made him highly critical of most federal programs, which he viewed as having been captured by powerful and self-serving constituencies that had converted the federal budget into "an automatic coast-to-coast soup line." While Reagan spoke reassuringly of shrinking government by combating "waste, fraud, and mismanagement," Stockman spoke of "starving the beast." While Reagan vaguely pledged not to include basic Social Security benefits in any proposed cuts, Stockman disparaged Social Security as "closet socialism" and "a giant Ponzi scheme," and he believed that many of its provisions — including COLAs and the payment of benefits to workers choosing to retire at 62 rather than at the normal retirement age of 65 — were fair game.

Moreover, Stockman thought that as a practical matter Reagan had no choice but to include some painful Social Security cuts in the proposals that his administration would take to Congress in the spring. As Stockman told the journalist William Greider: "If you don't do this in 1981, this system is going to land on the rocks, because you won't do it in '82 [a congressional election year] and by '83 you will have solvency problems coming out of your ears. You know, sometimes sheer reality has a sobering effect."

On May 12, 1981, the administration unveiled a package of proposed changes to Social Security that included a very sharp reduction in early retirement benefits — about 30 percent on average. Moreover, the cut was to take effect on January 1, 1982, less than eight months away. That meant that millions of workers already eligible for early retirement and on the verge of leaving their jobs would be affected. They would have no way to replace the retirement income they had been counting on — income that they would continue to forfeit, month after month, as long as they lived.

That had a sobering effect, although not the kind that Stockman intended. The public reaction was immediate and overwhelmingly negative. In the House, Democrats led by Speaker Thomas P. O'Neill, Jr., accused Reagan of a breach of faith and vowed to thwart him. His previously high public approval ratings plummeted overnight. Senior Republican lawmakers, most of whom had had no advance warning from the White House, were appalled. On May 20, Senate Majority Leader Robert Dole offered a resolution pledging that "Congress shall not precipitously and unfairly penalize early retirees." It passed by a vote of 96-0. Reagan withdrew his proposal the next day.

Skirmishing over the future of Social Security continued, however. The administration, cobbling together a comprehensive budget package in what would become the Omnibus Budget Reconciliation Act of 1981, continued to seek several changes, including the abolition of Social Security's minimum benefit, a provision dating from 1935 that was originally aimed at helping poorer workers then nearing retirement whose payroll taxes would not have contributed much toward their benefits. As time went on, the usefulness and relevance of the minimum benefit had become questionable, to the point where doing away with it might have been a reasonable step — except that it was being proposed by David Stockman, who wanted to eliminate the benefit for current as well as future beneficiaries. As a result, the minimum benefit became a major bone of contention between the administration and its critics during the summer of 1981. Hardly anyone fully understood the technicalities of the minimum benefit, but everyone could see that Ronald Reagan still seemed bent on altering Social Security.

The administration had been hoping that the House Ways and Means Committee would take the pressure off the White House by moving a Social Security bill of its own, and Representative J. J. Pickle, the conservative Democratic chairman of the Social Security subcommittee, was prepared to cooperate. On September 17, however, Tip O'Neill blocked Pickle from moving ahead. O'Neill was strongly opposed to cutting Social Security benefits. He also recognized that the controversy was working to the advantage of Social Security's defenders, and he wanted to force the White House to make the next move.

According to various accounts, it was either White House chief of staff James Baker or Senate Majority Leader Howard Baker who first suggested the idea of a bipartisan commission to President Reagan. Both saw that Social Security had become a huge liability for the president and would soon be a problem for Republican candidates in the 1982 mid-term elections. Clearly the solution was not to unleash David Stockman again or to issue more White House statements accusing Democrats of demagoguery. A bipartisan commission seemed attractive for several reasons: it would sideline the issue while the commission was deliberating; the members of the commission would be under considerable pressure to find common ground; and their consensus recommendations, if enacted into law in 1983, might or might not strengthen Social Security for the long run but with any luck would at least get it out of the spotlight before Reagan had to run for re-election in 1984. And if the commission failed, that would set the stage for reformers — whether genuine or with other motivations and agendas — to advance their own plans for Social Security's future.

On September 24, 1981, President Reagan went on television to deliver a speech addressing a wide range of economic issues. Toward the end, he turned to the topic bedeviling his administration. In order to "remove Social Security once and for all from politics," Reagan said, he would ask House Speaker O'Neill and Senate Majority Leader Baker to join him in appointing 15 members to a bipartisan task force charged with developing a plan "that assures the fiscal integrity of Social Security and that Social Security recipients will continue to receive their full benefits." Reagan, O'Neill, and Baker would each get to nominate five members of the commission.

In a follow-up letter to O'Neill, Reagan spelled out his proposal, which on its face seemed shrewd. Although the proposed structure of the task force was a bit complex — with each of the three appointers required to choose not just members of their majority party but also of the minority — the bottom line was that the Republican president and the Republican majority leader of the Senate would control two-thirds of the commission. That certainly seemed to increase the odds that the commission would be more disposed to favor benefit cuts than tax increases. Although several senior House Democrats balked at Reagan's plan, seeing the creation of such a lopsided commission as unnecessary and dangerous, Tip O'Neill accepted the president's challenge — and by mid-December the National Commission on Social Security Reform had become a reality.

To chair it, Reagan chose Alan Greenspan, the conservative economist who had headed the Council of Economic Advisors under President Ford. Although Greenspan had advised Reagan during the 1980 campaign, he had opted to remain in New York, overseeing his highly profitable economic consulting firm, rather than join the new administration. As commission chairman he would shuttle between Manhattan and Washington.

Reagan's other appointees were Robert Beck, chairman and CEO of Prudential Insurance; Mary Falvey Fuller, a California businesswoman; Alexander Trowbridge, president of the National Association of Manufacturers; and Joe Waggonner, a former congressman from Louisiana. Trowbridge and Waggonner were nominally Democrats, but both were conservative.

Howard Baker's appointees were Sen. William Armstrong, a conservative Colorado Republican who chaired the Social Security subcommittee of the Senate Finance Committee; Sen. Bob Dole, the powerful Kansas Republican who chaired the Senate Finance Committee; Sen. John Heinz, a moderate Pennsylvania Republican who chaired the Senate Special Committee on Aging; Lane Kirkland, president of the AFL-CIO; and Sen. Daniel Patrick Moynihan of New York, ranking Democrat on the Social Security subcommittee of the Senate Finance Committee.

Tip O'Neill's appointees were Rep. Bill Archer, a conservative Texan who was the ranking minority member of the Social Security subcommittee of the Ways and Means Committee; Rep. Barber Conable, a moderate New York Republican who was the ranking minority member on the Ways and Means Committee; Martha Keys, a liberal former congresswoman from Kansas; Rep. Claude Pepper, the very liberal 81-year-old chairman of the House Select Committee on Aging, who had represented Florida in the Senate in the late 1930s when Social Security was new and had ranked among its most outspoken advocates ever since; and Bob Ball, who had served as commissioner of Social Security under Presidents Kennedy, Johnson, and Nixon, prior to stepping down in 1973.

It was this group, consisting largely of people not favorably disposed toward Social Security, that was entrusted with developing recommendations for the program's future. Reagan instructed the commission to produce a report by January 1, 1983.

I NOW TURN TO THE GREENSPAN COMMISSION and the 1983 Amendments to the Social Security Act. The amendments, which largely followed the recommendations that were ultimately endorsed by the commission, constitute one of the most important developments in Social Security's entire history to date, and are still, as of this writing, the most recent changes of importance to the program. Yet no one who was on the inside of the negotiations has provided a thorough account of the remarkable process by which the amendments were actually arrived at. Alan Greenspan, for instance, devotes only a few paragraphs to the commission in *The Age of Turbulence,* his recent memoir.

Perhaps partly for this reason, the Greenspan Commission has provided grist for the kind of revisionist history that, if left unaddressed, may well create hazards for policymakers in the future. Was the commission really a great success? And is a bipartisan commission therefore the preferred mechanism with which to address the long-term financing challenge that Social Security faces today? Many politicians and commentators seem to think so. As I write, in 2007, several presidential candidates as well as numerous lawmakers and political commentators are enthusiastically on record in support of creating another Greenspan Commission.[1]

This is hardly surprising. After all, Alan Greenspan in his memoir describes the commission he chaired as "a virtuoso demonstration of how to get things done." Similarly, former White House chief of staff (and later secretary of state) James Baker in *his* recent memoir (*"Work Hard, Study... and Keep Out of Politics!"*) states: "The Greenspan Commission was a great success. It worked out a genuine compromise between those who wanted to increase taxes and those who wanted to reduce benefits."

But did it really? There is more to the story — much more.

First, some background. Until about 1977, the major events in Social Security's history had all been related to program improvements. The 1939 amendments, which added benefits for survivors and dependents, accelerated the effectiveness of the program by making it easier to earn eligibility for benefits and by initiating the payment of benefits in 1940 instead of 1942 as originally planned. The 1950 amendments, by extending coverage and greatly increasing benefits, made the program newly important for millions of workers and in so doing may in fact have saved social insurance

---

[1] *Editor's note:* Candidates continued to praise the Greenspan Commission during the 2008 presidential race. For example, during the Democratic primary debates, when Senator Barack Obama said he would not rely on a commission to address Social Security's long-term funding challenge, Senator Hillary Clinton responded: "With all due respect, the last time we had a crisis in Social Security was 1983. President Reagan and Speaker Tip O'Neill came up with a commission. That was the best and smartest way, because you've got to get Republicans and Democrats together. That's what I will do." [April 16, 2008] And during the second presidential debate, Senator John McCain, after stating flatly that Social Security benefits would have to be cut for future retirees, added: "Look, it's not that hard to fix Social Security. It's just tough decisions. Social Security is not that tough. We know what the problems are, my friends, and we know what the fixes are. We've got to sit down together across the table. It's been done before. I saw it done with our wonderful Ronald Reagan, a conservative from California, and the liberal Democrat Tip O'Neill from Massachusetts. That's what we need more of, and that's what I've done in Washington." [October 7, 2008]

The National Commission on Social Security Reform — all smiles (a rare occurrence). Front, left to right: Staff director Robert J. Myers, Rep. Claude Pepper, Martha Keys, Chairman Alan Greenspan, Mary Falvey Fuller, Rep. Bill Archer, Lane Kirkland. Rear: Robert A. Beck, Robert M. Ball, Alexander B. Trowbridge, Rep. Barber B. Conable Jr., Sen. John Heinz, Sen. Daniel Patrick Moynihan, Sen. Robert Dole, Joe D. Waggonner Jr. Missing: Sen. William L. Armstrong.

as an institution in the United States. The addition of disability insurance in the 1950s and of health insurance for the elderly — Medicare — in the 1960s, as well as the gradual extension of Social Security coverage to just about everyone who works whether as an employee or self-employed, all contributed to improving the program, as did the 45 percent increase in benefits between 1969 and 1972 and the replacement of ad hoc increases by automatic cost-of-living adjustments (COLAs) in 1972. These were all advances. The 1977 amendments, on the other hand, by incorporating changes that would trim future benefits, ushered in a period when Social Security was to prove largely defensive. The events leading to the 1983 amendments, and the amendments themselves, need to be seen against this background.

The Reagan administration took advantage of Social Security's looming crisis to propose cuts in benefits that were greater than needed to address the financing problem. Budget director David Stockman made several proposals to cut back on the protections provided by the program and might well have succeeded in getting them adopted if he had not included a proposal that caused a huge uproar, especially among those about to retire.

At the time, Social Security's normal retirement age — that is, the age of first eligibility for full benefits — was 65. Workers could, however, opt to begin collecting benefits as early as 62. If they did, their benefits would be reduced in an actuarially fair way — that is, at a level calculated to produce, on average, the same amount of lifetime payout. Stockman proposed to abandon the actuarial concept and to arbitrarily reduce the early retirement benefit by about 30 percent on average, with the change to take effect almost immediately.

Stockman "pitched the president hard," as Jim Baker recalls in his memoir, and Reagan approved Stockman's proposals after only a brief discussion and without the usual vetting by other administration officials. Baker, belatedly learning of Stockman's plans and anticipating the public reaction to the cut in early retirement benefits, launched a last-minute damage-control plan: Richard Schweiker, secretary of health and human services, would unveil the proposal — so that the TV cameras would be on him rather than on the president — and would frame it as "an HHS response to a congressional inquiry, not as a White House initiative." Baker also suggested announcing the proposal at the Social Security Administration's headquarters in Baltimore: "That would put as much distance as possible between the proposal and the president."

Schweiker dutifully made the announcement, but the damage-control strategy did not succeed. Millions of people who were about to retire were frightened and furious, and they promptly lit up the switchboards of their representatives in Congress, few of whom had known anything about the proposal before it was announced.

The planned cutback, leaked to the media on May 11, 1981, instantly became a big story. The next day I was about to be interviewed on network television when the reporter told me, off-camera, that he could hardly believe what was happening. He said that he himself had been planning to retire soon and that he and his wife were counting on augmenting their income with the benefits provided under current law. Although he tried to sound calm and objective while questioning me on the air, he was irate about the change, which he thought was totally unfair. His view was very widely shared. A week later the Senate passed a resolution intended to reassure the public that the plan would not become law, and the Reagan administration backed off.

A commission is born

But Social Security still faced a financing challenge, and after some additional setbacks the administration came up with a strategy to share the problem with the Democrats. Reagan sent a message to Tip O'Neill, the speaker of the House, proposing to create a National Commission on Social Security Reform, consisting of 15 members. The president would appoint five, including the chair, with no more than three to be from the same political party. The Senate majority leader would also appoint five, under the same ground rules. The Senate was in Republican hands, and the idea was that Majority Leader Howard Baker would appoint three Republicans, and then in consultation with Minority Leader Robert Byrd would appoint two Democratic senators. O'Neill would also appoint five members, three of his own choosing and two to be recommended by Robert Michel, the Republican minority leader.

This arrangement meant that while nominally the commission would be balanced, with eight Re-

REAGAN BACKS CUTS FOR SOME PROGRAMS IN SOCIAL SECURITY

CONGRESS TO GET PLAN TODAY

Early Retirement Penalty Would Be Raised, Tax Rate Reduced and Income Curb Eliminated

5|12|81

By STEVEN R. WEISMAN
Special to The New York Times

WASHINGTON, May 11 — President Reagan approved a package of proposed reductions in some Social Security benefits today. The intent is to preserve the solvency of the system and reduce Social Security tax increases scheduled to take effect in the next several years.

White House officials said that under the proposals, which are to be submitted to Congress tomorrow, the so-called early retirement penalty would be increased. This would reduce the minimum benefit granted to people retiring at age 62 to 55 percent of the benefit that would have been due them upon retirement at the age of 65. The current amount paid is 80 percent of the benefit due at the age of 65.

This step is designed to encourage workers to retire at the later age and not siphon money from the Social Security system. White House officials said the

publicans and seven Democrats, in fact the White House would control the appointment of ten of the fifteen members. The two Democrats subsequently appointed by the president, for example, were hardly your typical

Democrat: Alexander Trowbridge was the president of the National Association of Manufacturers and Joe Waggonner was a deeply conservative
former congressman from Louisiana. (Sandy Trowbridge turned out to
be a constructive albeit still conservative member of the commission. Joe
Waggonner was personally affable but conservative to the core — best
remembered today, if at all, as a diehard admirer of Richard Nixon who
had tried to talk Nixon out of resigning in 1974 — and he generally voted
to the right of most Republicans.)

Whatever the original White House strategy may have been, however,
in the end it wasn't the numbers that would count. The Republicans could
have exercised their two-thirds majority whenever they wished, providing they could agree among themselves (which they never did), but that
would have gotten them nowhere. What they needed was an agreement
with the House Democrats, led by the speaker. Without Tip O'Neill's
support there was no possibility of getting any amendments to the Social
Security Act through Congress.

O'Neill had been elected speaker in 1977. My relationship with him
really began not long after that, when some conservative Democrats
began advocating cuts in Social Security benefits as a way of restoring
the program to long-range balance. Previously I had dealt with O'Neill
from time to time while I was commissioner of Social Security, usually
when he contacted me on behalf of his Massachusetts constituents, but
we were not close. In the late 1970s, however, when Jake Pickle, chairman of the Social Security subcommittee of the House Ways and Means
Committee, began making various proposals to cut benefits, Tip stood
firm. He or his staff would call me for advice (or I would offer it without
waiting to be called), and I quickly realized that he was a stalwart supporter of Social Security.

At O'Neill's behest, I worked closely with two relatively junior members
of the Ways and Means Committee — Dick Gephardt from Missouri and
Jim Shannon from Massachusetts — whom he relied upon to keep Pickle
and other conservatives in line. At one point he had me meet with a large
group, the Democratic steering committee of the House, where I engaged
in something of a debate with Pickle, who wanted to increase the retirement age to 68 and was promoting that and other benefit cuts as the best
way to meet Social Security's long-term financing challenge. It was Dick

Bolling, chairman of the House Rules Committee and a very strong supporter of Social Security, who made sure that Tip and I connected again
in 1981, right after Reagan and Stockman launched their attack on the
program. I met with Tip and Ari Weiss, his chief domestic policy staff
person (whom Bolling extolled as "the nearest thing I've ever seen to
a legislative genius"), and discussed how to deal with the short-term
problem and how to bring the program into long-range balance without
compromising its principles. I found that on all important points we were
in complete agreement. When O'Neill appointed me to the commission,
he assured me that he expected to support whatever I came up with, and
he proved true to his word.

Alan Greenspan, named by Reagan to chair the National Commission on Social Security Reform, understood from the very beginning that
O'Neill had put me on the commission to be his proxy and that therefore
Greenspan needed to confer with me step-by-step as we went. And he
always did. Greenspan was also determined not to do anything that would
skew the proper functioning of the commission. Although he considered
the chances of getting to a consensus agreement to be poor, he did not
intend to have negotiations break down because of any feeling on the
Democrats' part that we were being treated unfairly. He deserves credit
for his fairness, especially since he was at heart a libertarian admirer of
Ayn Rand and philosophically unsympathetic to the whole idea of social
insurance.

The first meeting of the Greenspan Commission (as it was already
being called) was scheduled for February 27, 1982. Toward the end of
January, Greenspan phoned and invited me to join him for breakfast at
the Watergate Hotel, where he stayed when in Washington. With him
at this first of our many meetings were Robert Carlson, one of Reagan's
California aides who was the White House liaison to the commission, and
Bob Myers, who was to be the commission's staff director.

I had earlier greeted the suggestion of hiring Bob Myers as staff director
with enthusiasm, even though he and I often differed on substantive Social
Security issues. Bob was a conservative Republican, but he still seemed
to me a good choice. Back in 1934, before Social Security existed, he had
been hired as a junior actuary on the staff of the Committee on Economic
Security, helping to develop the cost estimates of the new program that

Roosevelt would recommend to Congress in 1935. Bob had then risen to become Social Security's chief actuary, serving in that role from 1947 until 1970. He was extremely knowledgeable and thoroughly competent from a technical standpoint. I thought he would be entirely dependable, and we could always raise a fuss if my expectations turned out to be wrong.

Meeting with Greenspan

Greenspan and I had never met, and I wanted to establish at the outset that I was indeed an expert, confident of my positions but also reasonable and helpful. I knew, of course, that the stakes were very high: Social Security really was running out of money — the first and only time that it has faced such an immediate short-term crisis — and I believed that this commission could be of critical importance to its future. Among other things I wanted Greenspan to understand that my intimate involvement in almost all of the major developments of Social Security in the past had thoroughly prepared me for a key role on the commission.

For some time prior to our meeting the White House had been putting out the word that Reagan did not want the commission to even consider tax increases. That stance infuriated the commissioners who had been appointed by Democrats. I told Greenspan that the administration's comments made it hard to believe that the commission was a genuine effort to address Social Security's problems. As Claude Pepper put it, Reagan might as well have named the panel "the National Commission on Cutting Social Security Benefits." I said that if the president wanted Democrats to take the commission seriously he should stop trying to tell us what we could and couldn't talk about. Greenspan agreed. He pledged that there would be no preconditions and that all options would be open for discussion.

Pursuing the point, I told him that we were also concerned about rumors that Stockman wanted the administration to push for benefit cuts after the 1982 mid-term elections regardless of what the commission might or might not do — reinforcing suspicions that the commission was nothing more than a device to get Reagan safely past the elections. In any case we were already having great difficulty seeing how a group with two-thirds of its members appointed by Republicans could reach a genuinely bipartisan agreement. Greenspan said that he understood our concerns and that he believed that the chances of success were less than even, but that he intended to give it a serious try. He said he did not intend to waste his time, or ours, on a phony exercise.

Greenspan then suggested that the commission should begin by discussing statements of philosophy: he proposed to write one for the conservatives and suggested that I write one for the liberals. I didn't like that idea at all.

"If we start out with philosophical or ideological discussions," I said, "I'm afraid we'll never get any further — we'll just get bogged down in irreconcilable differences and we'll spend all our time listening to polemics." I said that I thought the first task of the commission should be to try to establish a common understanding of the Social Security program and, if possible, to agree on the size of the problem we needed to address.

My proposal to begin with facts and figures appealed to Greenspan as an economist and as a pragmatist, and he dropped his idea about writing philosophical statements. But in making my proposal I had an additional purpose. I believed that a facts-and-figures discussion would effectively force the commission to accept, as a given, the present principles and structure of Social Security. Then its task would be limited to fixing the existing program. One

"One of my goals from the outset was to avoid letting the commission become a forum for proposals to radically alter Social Security's fundamental principles."

of my goals from the outset was to avoid letting the commission become a forum for proposals to radically alter Social Security's fundamental principles or weaken its ability to meet the nation's present and future needs.

We moved on to discuss the staffing of the commission. I asked Greenspan to allow the five of us appointed by Democrats to name three staff people of our own. He readily agreed, requiring only that all staff be under Bob Myers's general direction rather than designating our people as a separate minority staff.

I should pause here to note that the commission was very well served by its staff. Greenspan chose as his assistant Nancy Altman, an able young attorney who had been Senator John Danforth's legislative assistant. She was already familiar with Social Security but rapidly became an expert.

Her intelligence and objectivity were major assets, and her expertise has served the nation well ever since. (She has lectured at the Kennedy School of Government at Harvard, chairs the Pension Rights Center, is a leader of the National Academy of Social Insurance, and recently wrote a book — *The Battle for Social Security: From Roosevelt's Vision to Bush's Gamble* — which should be required reading for anyone who wants to understand the program. In my judgment, she would make an excellent Commissioner of Social Security.) Nancy did a fine job as liaison between Greenspan and me, and between Bob Myers and me — and was trusted, I believe, even by those members of the commission who had difficulty trusting each other.

Our subgroup of five chose as our three staff members Merton Bernstein, a professor at the law school of Washington University in St. Louis and a retirement policy expert with valuable Capitol Hill experience; Betty Duskin, the legislative director of the National Council of Senior Citizens; and Eric Kingson, a young professor at the University of Maryland School of Social Work. Mert was only part-time, flying in from St. Louis, but he had the grandest title: senior consultant. Eric had been recommended by Claude Pepper's staff on the House Select Committee on Aging, who were nervous about the prospect of having everything go through me and wanted to have someone on the staff who was answerable directly to Pepper. In practice, all three answered to all five of us who were appointed by Democrats. They helped me prepare materials for our caucus discussions and for discussions with the other commissioners, and throughout the term of the commission they worked on a minority report that we wanted to have ready if the commission was unable to agree on recommendations.

In addition, I had valuable part-time assistance from Lori Hansen, who had been a professional staff member for Senator Gaylord Nelson in his capacity as chairman of the Social Security Subcommittee of the Senate Finance Committee. (She later served as the Senate Democratic member of the Social Security Advisory Board, established in the 1994 law that made the Social Security Administration an independent agency.) I also had able part-time support from Betty Dillon, who had been my executive secretary for many years, and from Howard Young, a very capable actuary with the United Auto Workers.

Bob Myers had several people from the Social Security Administration assisting him. Bruce Schobel, an actuary, worked especially closely with him. Virginia Reno, an exceptionally able researcher who could always be counted upon to find the data we were looking for, later became — and still is — a key person at the National Academy of Social Insurance, where she serves as vice president for income security. And there were quite a few others from SSA. Carolyn Weaver, a Senate Finance Committee staff economist who was Bob Dole's assistant, took an extremely conservative view of Social Security — much more so than Dole — but handled his technical work well and later worked closely with the legislative staff responsible for drafting the Senate bill that embodied the commission's recommendations.

A *"demagoguerous"* issue

Thanks to its excellent staff and the fact that many of its members were already quite familiar with Social Security, there was never any question about the commission's qualifications. Early on in our deliberations, however, we had to revisit the question of our independence. Although Greenspan and I were in full agreement on that point, the Republican political establishment as a whole seemed not to have gotten the word. Early in May, the Senate Budget Committee wrote into the next year's budget an indication that our commission was expected to produce a net saving of $40 billion.[2] Those of us appointed by Democrats saw this as an obvious attempt to limit our authority and predetermine our conclusions. At the commission's third meeting, on May 10, Senator Moynihan very forcefully questioned why the Senate Budget Committee should have anything at all

---

2 *Editor's note:* Democrats on the Senate Budget Committee tried to remove the $40 billion in Social Security savings from the budget resolution, but failed on a straight party-line vote. During Senate floor consideration of the resolution, Senate Democrats offered two separate amendments to remove the $40 billion in savings. Both attempts failed on essentially party-line votes. The Democrats had succeeded, however, in keeping the Social Security issue in the forefront of the daily news for several days. House Republican leaders, painfully aware that the news was generating bad publicity in an election year, announced that they could not support a budget package that included any Social Security reductions. Senate Republican leaders then eliminated the $40 billion in savings from the budget resolution.

PENSION MEETING ENDS IN CONFLICT

Democrats Assail Republicans on Cuts in Social Security

5/11/82

WASHINGTON, May 10 (UPI) — Partisan conflict broke out today at a meeting of the National Commission on Social Security Reform over a Senate committee's budget blueprint urging $40 billion in retirement system savings.

The hourlong argument between the panel's Democratic and Republican members further eroded prospects that the committee could produce a unified and coherent report by its year-end deadline. Accusations of demagoguery punctuated the meeting, the panel's third, which was called to discuss private pension programs.

Senator John Heinz, Republican of Pennsylvania, tried to ease the dispute by announcing that he would introduce a resolution Tuesday that would separate Social Security spending from the overall budget. The proposal, an effort to remove discussions about the retirement system from the annual budget

to say about where we might come out. That prompted Senator Armstrong to respond with equal forcefulness, in what amounted to a personal diatribe against Moynihan. In the course of it he coined an adjective new to me, accusing Moynihan of trying to make Social Security "a demagoguerous issue from front to back and top to bottom," and things went rapidly downhill from there.

This was exactly the kind of acrimonious posturing that Greenspan and I had hoped to avoid. Fortunately, in the middle of it Senator Dole turned to the audience (the commission's meetings were public and televised by C-SPAN) and growled, in his deep voice and with his trademark wry tone, "I want to apologize to the non-congressional members of the commission. We carry on like this all the time on the floor of the House and Senate." Everyone laughed — except perhaps Armstrong, who was pretty hot by that time and in any case quite humorless — and we soon got back to the business at hand. But the incident was a reminder that we were always at risk of being derailed by partisan polemics.

In theory everyone on the commission had an equal voice. But in fact we were not all equal. Claude Pepper was at that time the most influential spokesman for older people in the country, and so he had, in effect, veto power over our deliberations. (He was also a fierce foe of Ronald Reagan, viewing him as "an affable man with foolish, dangerous ideas.") If Pepper had ended up taking the position that the commission's recommendations were contrary to the interests of older people, Tip O'Neill would never have been able to corral enough Democratic votes to move Social Security legislation to the floor of the House, let alone get it passed there and sent on to the Senate. Moreover, Pepper and Lane Kirkland, who represented the labor movement, had agreed at the outset that they would stick together.

Thus any recommendations that might emerge from the commission's deliberations would have to clear a double hurdle — winning the support not only of the chief spokesman for those receiving benefits from Social Security but also of the chief spokesman for those paying the payroll taxes to support those benefits.

There was one exception to this pact. Although there was broad support from the outset for the idea of extending Social Security coverage to federal employees, Kirkland made it clear that he could not support that, because the union representing them opposed such an extension — claiming that their existing civil service pension coverage might be compromised or that, in return for the added protection, they would have to contribute too much of their wages. Kirkland knew that these arguments were fallacious and that it was entirely reasonable for the commission to consider such a change, but he also felt bound by the AFL-CIO's policy of not taking positions at odds with any of its member unions. He let us know, however, that he wouldn't object to other commissioners supporting such a recommendation. So in this instance the Pepper-Kirkland pact did not apply. Otherwise the two were always in complete agreement, which gave them considerable leverage.

I became the key Democratic commissioner not by personal political affiliation nor even solely by relevant experience but because the House was in Democratic hands, and so Tip O'Neill was essential to arriving at an agreement with the president. He was at that time the most powerful Democrat in the country, and I was his representative. Moynihan, in contrast, was serving in a Republican-controlled Senate and had been appointed by Howard Baker at the request of Robert Byrd, the minority leader. Byrd felt compelled to appoint Moynihan because he was Social Security's chief advocate in the Senate and had chaired the Senate Finance Committee's subcommittee on Social Security, but Byrd was only lukewarm at best about the whole idea of having a commission, and moreover was not inclined to consult closely with Moynihan, who had never tried very hard to conceal his conviction that he was at least ten times smarter than Byrd. That they had a distinctly cool relationship was well known, and this further weakened Moynihan's position within the commission — although he was always a constructive participant, and also one whose Hibernian sense of humor got us over some rough spots. (In one meeting, when Barber Conable lost his temper and chastised Moynihan for engaging in "unconscionable blather," Moynihan smilingly accused Conable of making an ethnic slur.)

Martha Keys had been appointed by Tip primarily to represent the interests of women and had standing as a former member of the House Ways and Means Committee, but she had been defeated for re-election in 1978 and had then had a job in the Department of Education. She too was a constructive member of the commission but one with limited influence beyond her area of particular interest (which was to improve Social Security by adopting an earnings-sharing provision for married couples along with other measures to address disparities in the benefits received by women). However, the five of us — Pepper, Kirkland, Moynihan, Keys, and I — by managing to stick together had much more influence than would otherwise have been the case.

Generally speaking, the commission proceeded along the lines that Greenspan and I had agreed to. Our first goal was to try to bring the commissioners to some minimally equal understanding of what the program was all about and what the problem was. Beginning in February 1982 the commission met on a more or less monthly basis, and through that summer the meetings were largely informational and educational. Bob Myers had developed many useful materials, and he devoted considerable time to giving what were essentially long and somewhat soporific tutorials on Social Security's origins, evolution, objectives, and financing options. For the most part we steered clear of actually debating possible options, let alone attempting real negotiations, but with the help of Bob's seminars we did arrive at some tentative agreements on the facts.

Early on it became clear that we would have to exclude Medicare from our deliberations if there was to be any hope of getting anywhere. Robert Beck, president of Prudential and leader of the business group on the commission, wanted to lump Social Security and Medicare together, thereby hoping to convince the commission that the programs faced such huge combined costs that the only "solutions" were unacceptably high increases in payroll taxes, major infusions from general tax revenues, or very large benefit cuts. Of these he favored only the latter, of course, and he tried for quite some time to bring the commission around to his point of view. But Bob Myers's tutorials were useful in persuading commissioners that any possibility of solving Social Security's problem rested, at least initially, on separating it from consideration of Medicare.

Getting to the 1990s

As had been clear all along to those closely acquainted with the program, the real challenge was getting from 1983 — when it was estimated that the system would have insufficient funds to pay full benefits — to the 1990s. At that point, and for the next two decades, the financing of the system would become much easier to handle. This was because the people who would be becoming eligible for retirement benefits from the 1990s until about 2010 were part of the low-birthrate cohort of the 1930s. Meanwhile the number of people paying into the system would grow disproportionately, because their numbers would include the very high-birthrate cohort of the late 1940s and early 1950s, better known as the baby boomers. Thus revenues to the system would be increasing even as costs became more manageable.

As a spokesman for Save Our Security (SOS) — a coalition created in 1979 that consisted of about one hundred organizations representing labor, older people, the disabled, social welfare groups, and others — I had been arguing that it would make sense to allow the Social Security trust fund to borrow from the Medicare and disability insurance trust funds and then to pay the money back in the 1990s. When political commentators claimed, as they increasingly did, that Social Security faced "bankruptcy," I pointed out that it is hardly correct to say that someone with three bank accounts is facing bankruptcy if two of the accounts are solvent, as those funds were. I also argued that Social Security should be allowed to borrow money from general revenues if interfund borrowing should prove insufficient to get the system safely past the 1980s, again with a pledge to repay the loan in the 1990s. That would have worked perfectly well, but there was such widespread opposition to tapping general revenues that we could never get agreement on it, even within SOS. So it would obviously be a hard sell — truthfully an impossible sell — within the Greenspan Commission, although Bob Dole was actually in favor of it.

The conservatives on the commission did not necessarily disagree with our argument that the challenge was in getting to the 1990s, but they definitely disagreed with our view that the right way to get there was by increasing income. They wanted to cut benefits. We, however, believed strongly that benefits were by no means too generous, and that cutting them very much, even as a means of getting to the 1990s, simply could not be justified — particularly with private pensions increasingly in jeopardy.

Nevertheless it was clear to me from the beginning that if there was to be any hope at all of reaching an agreement, it would have to be based on coming up with something approximating an equal distribution of changes that could be identified as tax increases and those that could be identified as benefit cuts. The big question was how to get there.

First we needed to discuss the size of the problem. And to the great surprise of the commission's conservatives, our five-person caucus supported an estimate based on extremely pessimistic assumptions about the performance of the economy from 1982 to 1990. Those assumptions resulted in projecting a big short-term gap between income and outgo. The conservatives had expected us to do whatever we could to make the gap appear as small as possible so that it would be easier to close — at least on paper. But my view was that we as the defenders of the system had the most to lose if, after deliberating for nearly a year, we were to come up with a plan that then failed even to get us all the way to the 1990s.

Like many others, I had made assumptions in the 1970s that proved unduly optimistic, and I did not want to be in that situation again. Among other things, I was deeply concerned about the effect on public opinion of the recurrent waves of press accounts predicting Social Security's demise. The fact that perfectly reasonable financing options were readily available — such as borrowing from the other funds or from general revenues — never seemed to make it into the media's coverage, with the result that people were just seeing one scary headline after another and were rapidly losing confidence in the ability of the government to keep Social Security from "going broke." Among other things, the erosion of public confidence was creating opportunities for advocates of radical change to promote their schemes. I wanted to put an end to the doomsday forecasts. I wanted a big estimate of the short-term gap so that when we came up with a package of recommendations to close it we could be confident of reaching the 1990s and the safety of the next two decades. Indeed, I wanted to over-solve the problem if possible.

I also wanted the gap to be big enough so that it couldn't possibly be closed solely by making benefit cuts. If the target number was big enough it wouldn't be politically palatable for the Republicans to push for benefit cuts of the size that would be needed. They would have to accept tax increases as part of the solution.

"People were seeing one scary headline after another... I wanted to put an end to the doomsday forecasts... Indeed, I wanted to over-solve the problem if possible."

AP-THIS MORNING-TAKE 2
TOPIC: ELDERLY   12/1/82

IF THE SOCIAL SECURITY SYSTEM RAN ON CONFIDENCE, IT WOULD BE IN
EVEN WORSE SHAPE THAN IT IS NOW.
THREE OUT OF FOUR PEOPLE RESPONDING TO A RECENT SURVEY
HAVE LITTLE OR NO CONFIDENCE THAT THE SYSTEM WILL
PROVIDE THEM BENEFITS WHEN THEY RETIRE
ASSOCIATED PRESS AND N-B-C NEWS
STILL, 78 PERCENT
SOCIAL SECURITY.

Social Security Is

▶BROKE

Meaningful reform needed to save the system—now. 12/82
Grover Norquist

Within our caucus, except for Claude Pepper we all acknowledged from the outset that there would have to be benefit cuts of some sort if there was to be any hope of reaching agreement. But there was a severe limit on how much of the gap could be met by short-run benefit cuts. Realistically, we couldn't propose cuts to benefits already awarded or about to be awarded; that would have had us playing Stockman's game. Delaying the COLA or making far-off changes in the benefit formula were the practical limit for benefit cuts, and only a COLA delay would help meet the short-run deficit.

At the outset I had asked Bob Myers to produce a comprehensive listing of all possible changes with their short-term and long-term cost effects so that we would have something solid to work with in our deliberations. Bob had balked at first: he wasn't sure that a task of that magnitude could be accomplished in the time available, and because of our past difficulties he was predisposed to believe that my asking for such a list was proof that I had some sort of subterfuge in mind. (For many years he had accused me of being a Social Security expansionist; I suppose I thought of him as a contractionist.) Fortunately for me, Bruce Schobel thought that such a list was a good idea even if the idea did come from me, and he persuaded Bob to do it. The list proved very useful in helping everyone on the commission to appreciate the actual effects of various options.

As we continued to discuss the size of the problem there was a growing consensus that we needed to produce a net saving of $150 billion to $200 billion in order to get us to the 1990s. (As we refined our estimates the target became $165 billion.) A modest COLA delay would get us about $40 billion — obviously far short of what was needed if we were to meet the conservative members of the commission even roughly halfway. For a long time we were effectively stymied.

Circling the wagons — and keeping them together

Early on I decided to try very hard to keep all five of us together on our proposals and on writing a minority report if it came to that. So we always caucused before the meetings of the full commission and developed our positions. It was clear from the beginning that I was to operate as both our chief of staff and as our chief negotiator, charged with finding the right positions and, if possible, any accommodation with the other side. It was simply assumed that I would develop our agendas, direct our three staff people, and if necessary draft our minority report. We would frequently caucus in Claude Pepper's office, and I would always defer to him to chair the meeting, but he would invariably say to me, "Oh, no, you chair it."

This arrangement worked well until a time, some months along, when the staffs of some of the principals — not the principals themselves — became nervous about what I might be up to and felt that they were not being kept fully informed. This was indeed the case, and had to be: how many people can you negotiate with at the same time? Nelson Cruikshank, my long-time ally at the AFL-CIO, who was at this time directing research and education work for SOS, took me to lunch at the International Club to tell me of the staffs' uneasiness — particularly, as I recall, on the part of Charles Edwards on Pepper's staff at the Committee on Aging and Bert Seidman at the AFL-CIO. I told Nelson that I would do my best to keep everyone tuned in, but that to some extent the problem just couldn't be helped. In fact I was afraid of major participation by staff, fearing that some would be more intractable than the principals.

Meanwhile I was doing everything I could to build broad support for the idea of addressing Social Security's financing challenge within the commission if at all possible, rather than letting the commission expire with the issue still unresolved — at which point we would find ourselves watching helplessly from the sidelines as Social Security became a political football again in 1983. I was very concerned that if that happened we would completely lose control of the debate. Although the commission seemed to be going nowhere, I made it a practice to meet with individuals and groups to explain Social Security's financing problem and the possible solutions, trying whenever possible to move people in our direction.

I met, for example, with Senator Heinz and his staff, because he was the most liberal of the Republicans on the commission and the most open to exploring options. I also met with Barber Conable and his top staff person, Pete Singleton, to try to get his support for taxing Social Security benefits and the idea of coupling an acceleration of scheduled contribution-rate increases with a refundable tax credit (about which more later). I didn't get his agreement at that time, but our initial meetings led, I think, to his later willingness to accept these recommendations.

I met with Senator Russell Long, the ranking Democrat on the Senate Finance Committee, hoping to get his support for the kind of balanced package that we were groping toward. (He demurred, however, telling me bluntly and with some annoyance that the obvious solution was simply to raise taxes and that if he had known in 1977 that we needed more money he would have gotten it for us while the Democrats were still in the majority and he was chairing Finance.)

At Senator Max Baucus's request I had a three-hour meeting with him, which really was a basic tutorial on the nature of Social Security and all the issues related to it. He was then a junior member of the Senate Finance Committee, but it was a meeting that would pay dividends, both in the short term — because he made major contributions to the committee's deliberations prior to enacting the 1983 amendments — and in the long run, because as of this writing he chairs the Senate Finance Committee and has become an influential policymaker.

I met several times with Dan Rostenkowski, chairman of the House Ways and Means Committee, giving him the broad outlines of what we were talking about and where I thought we might end up. He took a supportive tone but made it clear that he did not expect the commission to succeed. He had little use for people who hadn't been elected, and he expected to have to resolve Social Security's short-term financing crisis within his committee in 1983. That worried me, because he was considered by many Democrats — especially O'Neill — to be entirely too deferential toward Reagan. I met with Jake Pickle, chairman of the Ways and Means subcommittee on Social Security (about whom O'Neill had the same concern), and, at O'Neill's request, I met several times with Barney Frank, already an influential liberal in the Democratic caucus.

I met often with O'Neill's key staff aides, Ari Weiss and Jack Lew. Both were quick studies who soon understood the structure, politics, and financing challenges of Social Security as well as anyone on Capitol Hill. They paid close attention to the commission's deliberations, offered valuable insights, and always kept O'Neill fully informed. (Jack Lew, with whom I developed a particularly close rapport, went on to head the Office of Management and Budget in the Clinton administration.)[3] I also met with Wendell Primus of the Ways and Means Committee, to whom Weiss and Lew looked for ideas and to vet any numbers under discussion. And, as noted above, I also spent time when I could with the personal staffs of the commissioners in our caucus, including Ed Howard and Richard Lehrman from Pepper's staff; Elise Ribicoff from Moynihan's staff; and Bert Seidman and Larry Smedley from the AFL-CIO.

I had lunch several times with Jodie Allen of the *Washington Post's* editorial staff and talked with her frequently on the phone, and the *Post* was consistently supportive of balanced solutions. I talked often with *Post* reporters Spencer Rich and David Broder and with Warren Weaver, Edward Cowan, Steven Weisman and other reporters at the *New York Times,* as well as with reporters covering the commission for the *Wall Street Journal, Los Angeles Times, Chicago Sun-Times, Baltimore Sun, Time,* and *Newsweek.* I

|0|17|81

Arguing Against Social Security Cuts

By WARREN WEAVER Jr.
Special to The New York Times

WASHINGTON, Oct. 16 — The vast majority of the 36 million Americans receiving Social Security checks have never heard of him, but Robert M. Ball is probably more responsible than any other individual for persuading Congress to ignore President Reagan and make only minor adjustments in the retirement system.

Senator Daniel Patrick Moynihan of New York and Speaker of the House Thomas P. O'Neill Jr. of Massachusetts, led the visible and audible resistance to Social Security change, but behind these Democrats and their allies, feeding them the critical statistics, has been this 67-year-old former bureaucrat and protector of the system.

A Careerful of Statistics

For all its political emotionalism, Social Security is an issue dominated by numbers, a country ruled by actuaries. For more than 30 years, Mr. Ball lived with those numbers, joining the Social Security Administration in 1939 as a fledgling field representative and ultimately heading it as commissioner from 1962 to 1973.

Thus, he had a careerful of statistics ready when President Reagan declared last May that the Social Security system was on the brink of bankruptcy. The President called for more than $50 billion in short-term economies with more to come later, most involving benefit cuts.

As Congress began nervously juggling the President's recommendations, its committees summoned Mr. Ball, the career administrator. His oft-repeated message: the immediate shortage in the Social Security fund is greatly exaggerated, and the short-term problem can be solved by merely permitting the retirement fund to borrow from the parallel Medicare and disability funds.

But President Reagan had also looked ahead some 35 years to the time when a shrinking work force may have to support a swelling retired population. The President wanted to start trimming benefits now to stave off such a 21st-century disaster; Mr. Ball argued that this would be premature.

The former head of the system ap-

---

3 *Editor's note:* Jack Lew is currently (2010) serving in the Obama administration as deputy secretary of state for management and resources.

also spent considerable time with TV reporters, particularly Dan Schorr, then with CNN, and ABC's Barry Serafin. Over time I had some success in changing the tenor of coverage by patiently explaining to reporters, as often and in as much detail as they could stand, why the sky wasn't really falling and how relatively modest changes could get Social Security safely through the difficult 1980s.

I encouraged Alicia Munnell, then with the Federal Reserve Bank of Boston (and subsequently co-founder with me of the National Academy of Social Insurance), to write on what to do about Social Security and what *not* to do, particularly to rebut Wall Street banker Peter G. Peterson, then as now a strident critic of the program and an unrelenting prophet of demographic doom. On substantive positions I consulted with Alicia and with Henry Aaron and Joe Pechman of the Brookings Institution along with many other experts. At my request Alicia testified before the commission to provide the facts about the decline of private pensions, countering — and demolishing — inaccurate claims that cutting back on Social Security could be justified because private pensions were growing and would provide a larger share of retirement income in the future. I asked Henry to testify before the commission as the Democratic coun-terweight to Stanford economist Michael Boskin, an early proponent of privatization schemes. Henry did an outstanding job and then expanded his testimony into an excellent Brookings publication on the economic effects of Social Security. (Joe Waggonner, meanwhile, made his most useful contribution by courteously dismissing Boskin's plan, "as good as it might well be," because, he said, it clearly went beyond what the com-mission could realistically consider in the time available. With that one casual comment he effectively swept privatization off the table.)

Outside groups played an important role in shaping public opinion, especially at the outset. SOS and other groups were particularly impor-tant in opposing Reagan's May 1981 proposals. Later it became more dif-ficult for them to support specific proposals when it became clear that there would have to be some sacrifices by beneficiaries and workers. I kept meeting with them, however, to explain the basis of various propos-als and to emphasize the desirability of arriving at solutions within the commission if at all possible. I conferred privately with Wilbur Cohen[4] on many occasions, and he fully supported the general approach that our caucus was taking.

I also met with AARP, but with no success. AARP's role — in which it ultimately ended up opposing the commission's recommendations, joining with Senator Armstrong and the National Federation of Independent Business in a strange-bedfellows alliance — struck me as odd indeed. AARP opposed just about every constructive proposal that emerged from the entire negotiating process. At one point Arthur Flemming, who had co-founded SOS with Wilbur Cohen, and I had lunch at the Hay-Adams Hotel with Cy Brickfield, AARP's CEO, and tried to persuade him to support the idea of raising revenues by moving up the date of the next scheduled payroll tax increase. He claimed that he saw the logic of it but that his hands were tied. AARP supposedly made policy on the basis of members' responses to questionnaires, and he said that his members didn't like the idea of moving up the contribution-rate increase. But we pointed out that AARP hadn't told its members that our proposal included an income tax credit to offset the impact of the payroll-tax increase, so he didn't know how his members felt about that. Brickfield then said, without much apparent conviction, that he would get his members' reaction to that, but nothing came of it. (In those days AARP was a real nuisance, essentially taking the position that they alone were the defenders of the elderly and needed no allies. Fortunately that stance had changed by the time George W. Bush came along: AARP supported my efforts to protect Social Security against Bush's campaign to partially privatize the program.)

I include this rather lengthy recitation of meetings to convey some sense of what was involved in trying to work with all those who felt that they had a claim on the outcome of the commission's work. I needed to bring as many stakeholders as possible on board and then try to keep them there despite all their misgivings about where we might be headed. Indeed

---

4 *Editor's note:* Wilbur Cohen (1913–1987), described at length elsewhere in Bob Ball's memoir, was a founder of Social Security and the principal architect of Medicare, and was appointed secretary of health, education and welfare by President Johnson in 1968. During the 1980s he devoted much of his time and his legendary energy to defending Social Security as co-chairman (with Arthur Flemming) of Save Our Security (SOS).

I spent so much time going to and fro, and in meetings, that Claude Pepper began calling me "the Habib of Capitol Hill" — a flattering reference to Philip Habib, the legendary roving ambassador, always airborne or so it seemed, who was then shuttling to and from the Near East, working to save Beirut and bring peace to Lebanon. Although Phil Habib's work was much riskier than mine, requiring him to meet with people whose main goal was to kill each other, there was one similarity. We both knew that even when the prospects of getting an agreement seem remote, an atmosphere of trust and shared information must be created and sustained if there is to be any hope of having everyone in the room and on speaking terms at the moment of opportunity — when and if that moment suddenly arrives.

It did not seem likely, how-ever, that the commission would experience such a moment. After about half a dozen formal meetings — and with the commission's expiration date rapidly approaching — we were really getting nowhere, other than having agreed on the size of the problem.

THE WALL STREET JOURNAL
Friday, December 10, 1982

Bipartisan Panel on Social Security Slates Meeting Today; Progress Isn't Expected

By ROBERT W. MERRY
Staff Reporter of THE WALL STREET JOURNAL
WASHINGTON—The Social Security De-   cost-of-living adjustment. He also recom-

A headline that could have run at almost any time in 1982.

We had been meeting mostly on Capitol Hill. Within the commission there was a feeling, which I shared, that it would be a good idea to hold the November meeting outside Washington, at a location where the commissioners, particularly those with busy offices on the Hill, might be less distracted by other commitments. I've heard that Greenspan tried to get us invited to the presidential retreat at Camp David (perhaps hoping that the Great Communicator would charm us into arriving at an agreement), but that someone at the White House balked. Whatever the facts, there were no indications that Reagan wanted to meet with us, and we ended up meeting for three days at a rather nondescript Ramada Inn in Alexandria, Virginia. That was certainly not as thrilling as being helicoptered to Camp David would have been, but it was at this meeting that we made the first serious attempt at negotiation.

Within our caucus there was agreement at this point that we would move ahead with proposals to cover newly hired federal employees (with

Kirkland dissenting) and to move up the payroll tax increase scheduled for 1990 to 1985, coupling it with a refundable tax credit for workers so that moving up the tax rate did not create any new burden on them. The refund had to be part of any plan that would have Kirkland's support. We also proposed to increase the tax on self-employed workers; to cover all newly hired state and local government employees; and to cover all non-profit employees. We were also prepared to offer several proposals for less significant changes such as crediting the trust fund for uncashed benefit checks and requiring the government to make additional payments to the trust fund to cover Social Security benefits for veterans (about which more later).

We also agreed to make a proposal that none of us liked: delaying the COLA by three months. That would be a significant benefit cut and a real concession on our part, one that would demonstrate our good faith and our willingness to negotiate.

I believe that by the time of the Alexandria meeting I was the only member of our five-person caucus who still thought that there was much chance for a real agreement within the commission, and I doubt that any of the other members of the commission, with the possible exception of Greenspan, held out much hope either. (For a few members, of course, the failure of the commission was the preferred outcome all along.) At Alexandria we were able to agree formally on the financing goal to be sought — in the short term, a net saving of $150 billion to $200 billion — as well as on Bob Myers's list of options and on several non-financial matters, but it seemed likely that this would be as far as the commission could go. Although our caucus's proposal would produce the necessary short-term savings, the Republicans would not support it. But they could not agree on a proposal of their own, so there seemed to be no way to avoid an ultimate deadlock — and the failure of the commission when the clock ran out.

A first stab at real negotiations

A few of us were still not quite ready to accept that outcome, however, and so at Alexandria we began trying to conduct negotiations behind the scenes. In public the commission discussed three proposals: ours; a very conservative proposal by Bob Beck relying almost entirely on benefit cuts; and an effort by Senator Heinz to get people to agree that as a matter of principle half the solution should come from raising taxes and half from cutting benefits, with the added notion that those who didn't want to cut benefits should design the cuts and those who didn't want to increase taxes should design the increases. None of these proposals generated much open support.

But at the same time it became increasingly clear that some people on the Republican side wanted an agreement badly enough to at least consider making some genuine concessions. This group included Greenspan, Dole, Conable, and Heinz — the pragmatic chairman and the three pragmatic members of Congress on the commission. (Of the remaining six, only the moderately conservative Trowbridge ever showed any real interest in finding common ground. Archer, Armstrong, and Waggonner never demonstrated any willingness to compromise at all on anything, regardless of the merits or the consequences.)

The major step forward toward real negotiations occurred when, sitting next to Bob Dole during our public session, I leaned over and asked him how he would react if we were to modify our proposal to include both a three-month delay in the COLA and a way to slow the growth of benefit costs in the long run by making a 5 percent reduction in replacement rates (that is, in the percentage of a worker's income that Social Security benefits would on average replace), with the latter change to take effect in 2020. Dole said he would react with interest. I then called our caucus together and told them of his response. They had already agreed that this would be a reasonable concession to consider and suggested that we call Tip O'Neill. He approved of the idea and suggested only that we should couple it with a modification of our COLA proposal to make the delay effective all at once rather than spreading it over three years, as we had initially proposed. Tip explained that Dan Rostenkowski thought that, since the money was needed now, the cut should come right away, and

---

11/15/82

Securing Social Security

By RICHARD REEVES

ALEXANDRIA, Va. – They began debating my future, and yours, probably, in a room at the Ramada Inn here last Thursday morning.

The first session of the 15-member National Commission on Social Security Reform began at 10:15 in the Washington Lee Room, a Ramada ballroom — a lot less grand than marble and wood-paneled congressional hearing rooms available just across the Potomac River in Washington. But this debate is too hot for Congress to handle right now. The commission session, chaired by conservative economist Alan Greenspan, was your basic Washington media event — 10 television cameras, 100 reporters and 50 demonstrators. The 50 demonstrators, whose average age was a lot higher than their number, circled outside the motel chanting: "No ifs, ands or buts, No Social Security cuts."

They rhymed in vain. There will be some cuts, perhaps only for future Social

that it actually would be less painful, both financially and politically, to make it all at once: otherwise the pain would be repeated with each cut. We quickly agreed. The idea made sense, and it was, of course, in our interest to try to accommodate Rostenkowski if we could, since Ways and Means would have to vet whatever the commission might come up with.

So with that change, I asked Bob Dole to meet privately with us, in a room above where the commission's public meeting was taking place. He did, and then conferred with Greenspan out in the hall. Greenspan was intrigued and said he would call Jim Baker, Reagan's chief of staff, which he did. But there the idea stalled. Greenspan reported back that Baker thought our caucus had not made nearly enough concessions, and that in any case Social Security issues had not yet been addressed in the budget discussions that were then under way within the administration. That was a puzzling response. My guess is that Baker did not yet have control of the issue within the White House, but whatever the actual reasons may have been for the administration's refusal to engage us, it was a blow. Dole said, not unreasonably, that without interest on the part of the White House we would be unlikely to make much headway. So nothing came of what might have been our breakthrough proposal at Alexandria. But the effort was still worthwhile, because it was at this point that Dole and some of the other commissioners began to see at least a glimmer of hope in finding a real solution.

Greenspan, meanwhile, told reporters that he was encouraged about what we had already accomplished. He suggested that if the commission did nothing more than agree on the size of the problem, embrace the idea of covering newly hired federal employees, and develop a data base concerning possible changes, we would have made an important contribution to addressing Social Security's problems.

This was, to put it mildly, a stretch. But Greenspan was obviously sending up a trial balloon, hoping that the commission could at least save face if this was as far as we went. For my part, I felt that we would have failed — period. But I had long since realized that hardly anyone thought we were going to go much further. Moreover, many lawmakers continued to see the commission as nothing more than a device to get Reagan past the elections, at which point he and his adversaries would press their own views. So it wasn't surprising that Greenspan was searching for the silver lining on what certainly seemed to be a very dark cloud. But then rather suddenly the cloud began to look a bit less grim.

In the weeks just prior to the mid-term elections, the indefatigable Claude Pepper, after celebrating his 82nd birthday, had taken time off from his other commitments to campaign vigorously in some two dozen states. In many of them he was quite successful in pinning on Reagan the entire blame for any uncertainties about Social Security's future. He helped engineer a net gain of 26 Democrats in the House, many of whom were elected largely on the Social Security issue. That certainly strengthened our hand. It meant, at the very least, that some of the Republicans on Capitol Hill and in the commission would have to think twice before taking a hard line on Social Security in public, which in turn meant that to get an agreement we might not have to cut benefits further than we had already proposed.

On the other hand, we came back after the elections with time running out. The commission was scheduled to terminate on December 31. With the

Ronald Reagan's hopes of sidelining Social Security until after the 1982 elections did not pan out. Rallies in many key states — and Claude Pepper's barnstorming — helped elect a net gain of 26 Democrats in the House.

exception of our brief, behind-the-scenes effort at Alexandria, we had been getting nowhere in our formal meetings (and our December meeting lasted only a few minutes). Among other things, Pepper's inflammatory campaign attacks against Reagan had had the effect of making his most adamant foes within the commission — particularly Archer and Armstrong — even less interested in finding common cause. Then two good things happened.

A meeting that never took place

The first was a mid-December phone call to me from Dick Darman. I had gotten to know him in 1972, during the Nixon administration, when as a young assistant to Elliot Richardson (who was then secretary of health, education and welfare, and thus my boss) he had interceded to help me stop Chuck Colson (Nixon's special counsel and political hatchet man) from forcing us to include with Social Security's October benefit checks — just weeks before the election — a red-white-and-blue stuffer giving Nixon credit for that year's 20 percent benefit increase (which he had actually opposed) as well as the new cost-of-living adjustment. Social Security mailings had never before been used for such partisan political purposes, and I had no intention of letting it happen while I was the commissioner. I had threatened to resign, and Darman had gotten the White House to back off. Starting with that encounter, we had developed a relationship of mutual trust and respect.

Dick now had the title of assistant to the president and was Jim Baker's deputy. On the phone he asked: "Can we have a meeting that never took place?" I said sure, and on December 17 he drove over to see me — parking at some distance from my office and walking the rest of the way. I'll return to our secret meeting in a moment. (After the 1983 amendments passed, we agreed that the meeting no longer needed to be off the record.)

The second good thing was that Bob Dole submitted a very timely and constructive op-ed to the *New York Times*. It was published on January 3, 1983 — the very day when the new members of Congress were being sworn in. By that time Reagan had agreed to extend the life of the commission, but only until January 15. Meanwhile the Democratic victories in the mid-term elections had prompted many commentators to opine that the White House and the new Congress were inevitably facing legislative gridlock. Dole rejected that view, arguing that "the issues confronting us present as much opportunity as peril."

He continued: "Social Security is a case in point. With 116 million workers supporting it and 36 million beneficiaries relying on it, Social Security overwhelms every other domestic priority. Through a combination of relatively modest steps, including some acceleration of already scheduled taxes and some reduction in the rate of future benefit increases, the system can be saved."

There are various versions of what happened next. My understanding is that Moynihan, after reading Dole's op-ed at his desk on the Senate floor, walked over to compliment him on it. Moynihan later recalled saying to Dole, "Are we going to let this commission die without giving it one more try?" The two of them then phoned me. I had read Dole's op-ed that morning and had, of course, noted the key sentence, which sounded like something our caucus could have written. Yes, I said, it's worth a try.

The three of us met together for an hour or so and then phoned Greenspan, who promptly agreed to join us. We all knew, of course, that the commission as a whole was paralyzed, and I think we were all of one mind that the only way we could proceed at that point was by convening a small group of pragmatic people who knew how to negotiate and could put partisan rhetoric aside. Moynihan, when not in the limelight, could do that, but we also needed somebody solid from the House side, so we called Barber Conable, who had always been open to working out a balanced solution that would leave Social Security fundamentally intact. He agreed to join us. That made five of us from the commission who were willing to make one last try — very unofficially. We called Jim Baker at the White House, and he immediately invited us to meet with him at his house on Foxhall Road in Washington.

By this time the administration was hard at work on its next budget, and the numbers were not adding up to anyone's satisfaction. Reagan's pledge to balance the budget while simultaneously slashing taxes was not working out. Stockman was once again looking to Social Security to help close the gap between revenues and outlays, and Baker and Darman were, of course, very anxious to avoid doing anything that would create another presidential public relations fiasco. They were also convinced that the president would catch most of the blame if Social Security was allowed to run so low on funds that benefit checks had to be delayed. With that day only a few months away, the prospect of 36 million beneficiaries exacting revenge at the polls in 1984 must have been more than a little unsettling to the White House. Pragmatic proposals such as accelerating the scheduled payroll-tax increase and postponing the COLA — the essence of what our caucus had been advocating, reflected in Dole's op-ed — now looked more appealing.

> *"The prospect of 36 million beneficiaries exacting revenge at the polls in 1984 must have been more than a little unsettling to the White House."*

We met for the first time as a group on January 5, 1983. Accompanying Jim Baker at that meeting, and at subsequent ones, were Dick Darman, David Stockman, and Ken Duberstein, who served as the White House liaison with Congress. Baker and Darman were the negotiators. Stockman's role was limited to analyzing numbers. Duberstein never said anything during the negotiations but made it his task to report to the people on the Hill who needed to know what was going on — particularly Dan Rostenkowski, who as chairman of Ways and Means wanted to keep his options open and also wanted, if possible, to accommodate the White House (a willingness that continued to make O'Neill nervous).

I think it's fair to say that the necessary groundwork for this meeting had been laid when Dick Darman and I had our secret meeting at my office. Prior to that, Sandy Trowbridge had been making some eleventh-hour efforts at finding a compromise. Using Bob Myers's list of options, he had been drawing up a series of one-page plans, which he would circulate to the commission members and send over to the White House. All of his plans emphasized benefit cuts and none of them came close to what we considered acceptable, but apparently that hadn't been communicated to Reagan. As I learned on December 17, the president had looked at the sixth of Trowbridge's plans, under the misimpression that we had already agreed to it, and had actually marked it up in the margins with suggestions about moving some of its provisions even more in his direction. Dick showed

me the president's neatly handwritten notes. It's often said that Ronald
Reagan was averse to details, but as I looked at his notes I could see that
in this instance he was clearly paying close attention.

I explained to Dick that Trowbridge, although nominally a Democrat — he
had served as secretary of commerce in the Johnson administration — had
never been part of our caucus within the commission and was freelancing his
proposals. They included permanently weakening the COLA and raising the
retirement age to 68 — changes that were totally unacceptable to our caucus.
Dick was a bit chagrined by this evidence that he and Jim Baker were not
quite as on top of our negotiations as they had thought, but he recovered
quickly, and over the next two or three hours we had an exhaustive discussion of where things stood within the commission and within the administration. As soon as he left, I dictated a long memo on our meeting.
I want to paraphrase some of the main points here to convey a sense of
where things stood on December 17 and how much ground remained to
be covered if there was to be any hope of reaching an accommodation that
would be acceptable to the only two people who really mattered: Ronald
Reagan and Tip O'Neill.

- Dick told me that whatever I had heard about Reagan's opposition
  to tax increases was an understatement. He said the president was
  fanatical on the subject because of his experience as a movie actor.
  The president claimed to have known actors who would do a picture
  and then stop working because their income was so heavily taxed. I
  had never heard of such an actor, but even if the story was apocryphal
  the president wholeheartedly believed it. So it was a huge concession
  for Reagan to consider tax increases as part of a Social Security fix.

- In the short run the main argument would be over numbers, not
  principle, since the president was in fact open to some increase in
  taxes and we were open to some postponement of the COLA. But
  the differences over numbers were still enormous. And in the long
  run there remained a real difference in philosophy, with Reagan determined to scale back the scope of Social Security while we were
  equally determined to preserve it. I asked Dick if he thought it would
  be worthwhile to try to work toward an agreement on the short run
  and allow differences about the long run to be fought out in Congress.

He was doubtful, explaining that the president thought in terms of trading — he'd accept some things he didn't like in the short run if he thought he could get what he wanted in the long run.

- The president wanted to cut benefits by making a major change in the COLA. I suggested that in addition to delaying it by three months (as had already been discussed within the commission) we might consider a one-month further delay in 1984 and in 1985, then moving it to January in 1987 and putting it on a calendar-year basis thereafter. Dick thought this would be not nearly enough — that the president might want something like basing the COLA on the Consumer Price Index minus 3 percent for several years. That, of course, would have amounted to a big benefit cut, as well as substantially undermining the ability of the COLA to maintain the buying power of the benefits — its whole purpose.

- Within our caucus we had been talking about providing for fail-safe tax-rate increases in the next century if triggered by some mechanism such as Social Security's trust fund dipping below a certain point. Dick thought that getting such a provision past the president would be out of the question — that Reagan's main goal was to see the program scaled back in the future, and that he'd accept tax increases in the short run only in exchange for program cuts in the long run. That was his trading approach.

- Trowbridge's plan included raising the normal retirement age from 65 to 68 — among other things the equivalent of an across-the-board benefit cut. Dick said he couldn't understand why we were so opposed to that change, given that people are living longer. I explained that (1) the very people with the least faith in the system — young people — would be expected to pay into it longer at higher rates only to get less in benefits than now; (2) workers in heavy industry and manufacturing tended to view early retirement very differently than people with satisfying and physically undemanding white-collar jobs; and (3) a period of layoffs and high unemployment, such as the recession we were currently in, was hardly an auspicious time to propose keeping people in the labor force longer. I indicated, however, that it might be possible to discuss an incentive approach to make retiring after 65 more attractive, and that maybe for the long run it might be possible to consider an increased penalty for retiring before 65 but without changing benefits payable at 65.

- We discussed the possibility of taxing the benefits of higher-paid workers, based on the rationale that although Social Security is supported by a combined employer-employee contribution, only the worker's contribution is taxed (the employer's contribution being treated as a pre-tax business expense), and thus only one dollar of each two benefit dollars is taxed. Dick saw the logic of this idea (which I discuss further below) but thought that the president would see it as a tax increase, even though I pointed out that it could just as well be thought of as a benefit cut for the higher-paid. The one ray of hope, Dick said, was that the president often said he could see no reason why he and his wealthy friends were getting Social Security benefits — so he *might* be open to talking about taxing those benefits.

- I mentioned taking Social Security out of the unified budget, and he agreed that the idea had merit. Stockman would oppose it, he said, but more for institutional than intellectual reasons. (As director of the Office of Management and Budget, Stockman had a vested interest in keeping Social Security within the unified budget so that he could show proposed cuts to the program as improving the federal deficit, notwithstanding Social Security's separate funding.)

- From our conversation it was clear to me that there were deep differences within the White House about how to resolve both the substance and the politics of the Social Security financing challenge. Baker and Darman wanted to reach a settlement within the commission if possible and had persuaded the president that such a strategy made sense. They were concerned that it might be to the Democrats' advantage in the short run not to settle the issue, and that failure to reach an agreement would hurt Reagan in 1984 — but would also endanger Social Security, generating repercussions that no one would be able to control. Stockman was apparently on board, as were presidential counselor Ed Meese and Domestic Policy Council head Ed Harper, but purely for political reasons, not because of any abiding interest in Social Security. On the other hand, Martin Feldstein, chairman of the Council of Economic Advisors, had long been critical of the program, and Darman made it clear that Feldstein would welcome an open fight about its future. He told me that Feldstein and some others on the staff were urging Reagan to go on television and make an all-out attack on Social Security. Philosophically Reagan might have found that idea appealing, but his approval ratings were low, he would soon face a re-election campaign, and he knew that it was not in his interest to alienate millions of voters by trying to turn back the clock on all that had been accomplished through Social Security. Still, Darman thought it possible that if the commission failed and if the president then found himself in a renewed battle with Tip O'Neill, he might well launch a campaign to try to convince the nation that Social Security should be scaled back or even phased out. (That this was a real possibility rather than a strategic bluff was borne out when I later learned that Reagan said to Trowbridge, even as we were wrapping up negotiations in January 1983: "Isn't there some way we can make Social Security voluntary?")

My long meeting with Dick Darman left me with mixed reactions. On the one hand, it was clear that there was a great gap between what we in the caucus wanted for Social Security and what the White House wanted to accomplish. On the other hand, it was obvious that Dick had not just dropped by on his own for a friendly but inconsequential chat. When he left, he said he would see whether there were any more concessions that they could make, and I was optimistic that he and Baker would follow through. Indeed, they may well have had a role in the preparation and timing of Bob Dole's op-ed, his supposedly spontaneous encounter with Moynihan on the Senate floor, and their phone call to me.

Darman was good at making things happen — or not happen, depending on the situation. Jim Baker in his memoir describes Darman as someone "who could direct traffic through the intersection of policy and politics as well as anyone I ever met." He was also able to *stop* traffic at that intersection, as for example when he thwarted Charles Colson, a man who took pride in being valued by President Nixon for his ruthlessness. Darman himself acquired a reputation for treating people in a high-handed manner, and he has been described by Martin Anderson, another of Reagan's inner circle, as "easily the most disliked man in the White House."

But he was not high-handed with me, nor did I dislike him. We got along well. He was very self-assured, but he was also very competent and, as I had learned in 1972 and was about to find out again in 1983, when he committed himself to a course of action he could be counted upon to follow through. Later, during the presidency of George H. W. Bush, when Dick directed the Office of Management and Budget, he was probably the most powerful person in government next to the president. He was untroubled by conservative attacks accusing him of being a pragmatist rather than a reliable ideologue (a charge also leveled at Baker); he believed in getting things done, and in spite of our having quite different viewpoints, I was sorry when he left the government.[5]

When we began meeting at Baker's house on January 5, Baker and Darman did the talking from the White House side, and I did most of the talking for our little group from the commission. The commission as such, of course, was no longer functioning. Some of its members didn't know we were meeting. None of the staff were present. We were just a group of people who wanted to see whether we could get somewhere.

By that time Stockman had long since gotten into trouble for talking too candidly about the politics of the budget process to Bill Greider of the *Washington Post,* who had written it all up in a famous article for *The Atlantic,* and my impression is that Baker had him on a short leash. (Tip O'Neill's biographer later quoted Stockman to the effect that Baker had been prowling the White House corridors "as if armed with a bazooka, ready to blow up any budget proposal that had cuts in Social Security." Although that is factually off the mark, I like the image.) Stockman's role was limited to discussing with me the dollar amounts associated with various options, and we were generally in agreement. Greenspan, Dole, and Conable also said very little on their side, and Moynihan said very little on ours. I was somewhat surprised that Moynihan had so little to say. I get the impression from Baker's memoir that on one occasion, at least, he stayed on and chatted with Baker over drinks, but during our negotiations he said almost nothing. Sometimes, when we were taking a break, he would chat with me, but usually about some subject such as the history and architecture of Pennsylvania Avenue, which was one of his passionate interests.

---

5 *Editor's note:* Dick Darman died on January 25, 2008, four days before Bob Ball's death. Darman was 65.

Down the slippery slope...

At Baker's house we initiated ten days of real negotiations between the president of the United States and the speaker of the House of Representatives, with Baker and me as their proxies. It is important to understand that this was a total reversal of the usual commission or advisory council process, in which the goal is to arrive at consensus and develop recommendations that can then be taken to the principals. Here the goal was to come to an agreement acceptable to the two principals and then get the commission to endorse what had already been decided.

This point seems to have been lost on everyone who sees the Greenspan Commission as an unqualified success and as a model for the future. The reality was that the commission as such had just about struck out by the end of its originally appointed term in 1982, having reached agreement on nothing more than the size of the problem and the desirability of extending Social Security coverage to newly hired federal employees.

"The reality was that the commission as such had just about struck out."

Our self-appointed negotiating group began meeting in secret, but soon reporters found out that something was up. On January 7, one of the wire services reported that our group was going to be meeting during the weekend at a member's house outside Washington. That was an error — we were going to be meeting again at Baker's house, which was definitely within the District of Columbia — but since I was the only member of the group living outside Washington, assignment editors decided to stake out my house in Alexandria, and reporters started showing up there before dawn on Saturday. When Doris and I looked out the window, there they were.

I didn't know what to do. If I got in my car to drive to Baker's house, the reporters would follow me there. Doris tried to throw them off by going outside dressed in a sweatsuit, hoping they would conclude that she wouldn't be so informally garbed if we were about to host an important meeting. But they didn't take the hint. They sat in their cars and watched the street in front of our house.

Behind our house was a wooded area and a steep slope with the George Washington Parkway below. I called Dick Darman, explained the problem, and asked if he could send a White House car for me. He said he could, and I asked him to have the driver park on the shoulder of the parkway below our house. Then I waited a few minutes before quietly sneaking out the back door and heading down the slope. The ground was covered with snow, so the footing was tricky. I slipped and slid a few times but made it to the bottom without falling, and the White House car was waiting for me. I can truthfully state that this was the only time I've ever had to deceive the press, let alone so melodramatically.

When we began meeting at Baker's house I quickly realized that he and his colleagues had much lower expectations than I did. They weren't really expecting to come up with a set of detailed recommendations that could be agreed upon and put to the whole commission. They were thinking more of arriving at some points of agreement and a statement of differences, rather than developing a total plan, and they were assuming that whatever we produced and the commission accepted would then be put before the Congress, with the final negotiations to take place between the Congress and the White House.

I found this approach thoroughly unsatisfactory and explained why. I said I thought that if all the effort expended on convening a commission and holding meetings for a year was going to amount to anything worthwhile, we had to try to arrive at a single set of recommendations. Otherwise we would not have accomplished anything more than the commission had already achieved, which wasn't much. I said I thought we should take the time to review various proposals in detail and see what we could do. Baker and Darman were doubtful but at least open to the idea — they could certainly see the appeal of not getting into another bruising battle with O'Neill — and so we started down that road.

They started, however, from pretty far over to one side of it, with just about all of their emphasis on benefit cuts. On the COLA, for instance, they started with the equivalent of a three-year suspension. Before we were through, we were able to whittle that down to a six-month delay. That would be a permanent benefit cut, of course, but it was really the main concession that we ended up making toward benefit cuts.

I knew from talking with Darman in December that the White House was willing to consider some concessions on tax increases, mainly in the form of moving up the effective date of payroll tax increases that were already scheduled, but I also knew that a benefit cut reducing Social

Security's short-term costs by $40 billion and a tax increase producing about $40 billion in additional revenue wouldn't get us close to where we had to go. After all, we had to achieve a net savings of around $165 billion if we were to get Social Security safely to the 1990s.

Rather than limiting ourselves to conventional changes that would fit neatly into one box or another — tax increases or benefit cuts — we needed some proposals that would expand our horizons. So I began pushing hard for something that I had favored for many years but for which I had never been able to generate much support: the income taxation of Social Security benefits, with the revenue to be deposited back into the trust fund.

Taxing Social Security benefits was not a new idea. It had originated during the Kennedy administration, when Stanley Surrey, the assistant secretary of the treasury for tax policy, initially proposed it, early on in my tenure as Commissioner of Social Security. Stan Surrey was one of the nation's leading tax experts, totally devoted to making the income tax as fair and progressive as possible. He believed that Social Security benefits should be subject to income taxation because half of the contributions — the half paid by employers — had escaped taxation at the time, since employers could take those contributions from pre-tax income. His argument was that half of the benefits received should thus be subject to taxation, relying on the progressive structure of the income tax to ensure that the benefits of lower-income beneficiaries would not be taxed.

This was the way private pension benefits were treated, with the amount of the benefit that exceeded the employee's contribution subject to income taxation. And there was a strong case to be made that Social Security benefits should have been treated the same way from the start. The main reason they weren't was because of some early rulings by the Treasury Department that treated the collecting of Social Security revenues and the paying of benefits as unrelated activities, with benefits thought of as gratuities, which weren't taxable.

Many people were surprised when I as Social Security Commissioner supported Stan Surrey's position during testimony before the Ways and Means Committee in 1967. My reasoning was simple. In the first place, Stan was right on the merits. Secondly, and just as importantly, I knew that the more Social Security was treated like wages and private pensions, the more it would be considered an earned right rather than welfare. This was a very important distinction for workers and policymakers alike to make. You don't pay income taxes on something you haven't earned.

Stan Surrey's proposal went nowhere at the time. It was immediately and unfairly attacked by labor organizations and senior citizen groups, who accused him of advocating an excise tax on everyone's Social Security benefits. That, of course, was not what he was proposing, nor would I have supported such a tax. But it was not easy — then or now — to get most politicians and reporters to understand a tax proposal well enough so that they in turn can explain to their constituents and readers why it is fair and reasonable. (With ongoing support from the White House, Stan would have pursued the idea. But when Nixon came to power he saw the writing on the wall, left the government, and returned to teaching tax law at Harvard Law School.)

Some years later, when I tried to revive Stan's idea, I sought to avoid misunderstandings and unfair attacks by proposing to have the provision apply only to people who had dollar incomes above specified levels, so that the result would be the same as letting the progressive income tax work its will. My point was to make it absolutely clear that we did not propose to tax the benefits of lower-income people.

This sensible approach was recommended by the 1979 Social Security advisory council, chaired by Henry Aaron, but it was promptly torpedoed by the Senate, which passed a resolution proclaiming that Congress would never tax Social Security benefits. Nevertheless I brought up the idea again during the first meetings of the Greenspan Commission and had been trying to promote it ever since. But no one on the commission who had to run for elective office wanted to touch it. Although Dole and Conable were generally open to new ideas (or old ideas that were still new because they hadn't been tried), they both said to me, in effect, "Well, it may be a sensible enough idea, but it would never get passed. *Nobody* is going to vote for taxing Social Security benefits. So forget it."

I didn't forget it. I brought it up again in January 1983, at a time when the negotiators really needed the money, and this time they accepted it — proving to me never to say never, because it is always possible under the right circumstances to get agreement on almost any sensible proposal. This one would become a key provision in the agreement that would be accepted by Reagan and O'Neill, with the majority of the elected officials on the commission ending up in favor of it even though they had all said flatly that it would never pass. There was a lesson in that.

A benefit cut ... or a tax increase?

The genius of this proposal was that it could be characterized as either a benefit cut or a tax increase. Those who favored tax increases could say that this was a tax increase, and it certainly was. But those who favored cutting benefits could say that it was a cut in benefits. (A purist might also claim — and Senator Armstrong did — that it was also a back-door way of tapping general revenues for Social Security, since one could argue that the revenue from taxation of benefits should go to the Treasury rather than into Social Security's trust fund. But pragmatism tended to trump purism at this point.) We estimated that taxation of benefits would yield about $30 billion in revenue in the short term. It thus became very important — really essential — to arriving at an agreement.

" ...Or we could jettison some baggage. Or start the bilge pumps, or send an SOS... Well, let's call for some tea while we think about it "

By the end of 1982 the Greenspan Commission was widely regarded as a useless, time-wasting exercise, as this cartoon suggests.

Our little group also discussed — and ended up agreeing to recommend — several changes that we scored as improvements in the equity of the program rather than as benefit cuts or tax increases. For example, we discussed the fact that self-employed workers were currently not paying as much for their Social Security protection as employed workers were paying — that is, they were paying the employee's share but not the employer's, which meant that everyone else was paying somewhat more. We agreed to recommend that the self-employed should pay the double rate but be allowed to charge half of what they paid as a business expense, which would parallel the treatment of the employer's share of the payroll tax. That change would produce a significant amount of income for the program — about $18 billion in the short term.

There were several lesser changes that could also be scored as correcting inequities. For example, although employers and employees made contributions toward Social Security benefits with every payroll, the actual revenue from those wage deductions might not reach Social Security for some time. Meanwhile, however, Social Security was paying all benefits on the third day of the month. By crediting contributions the same way — that is, when deducted from wages rather than when the revenues were actually received — contributions would build up and earn interest faster and the trust fund would not have to keep as much money in reserve.

There was a similar problem with military service wage credits. Since 1957, members of the armed forces had received Social Security coverage, but the government did not pay anything to Social Security until the former member of the armed forces started collecting a benefit. That was unfair to civilian employers. Moreover, the government had been basing military service payments to Social Security primarily on the low nominal wages of service personnel, without fully taking into account the value of room and board. To correct for such past inequities we recommended the payment of a lump sum to the trust fund.

A similar issue concerned the failure of beneficiaries to cash their Social Security checks. Hundreds of thousands of uncashed checks had never been declared void, and so were still carried on the trust fund's books. I suggested that checks uncashed after more than six months should be voided and the fund credited for their value.

In the great scheme of things these items may not have seemed important, but straightening them out meant gaining significant income. Fixing the problem of military service wage credits alone would improve revenues by almost $18 billion in the short term. Crediting the fund for uncashed checks was worth nearly $1 billion. All told, these changes would net about $165 billion between 1983 and the 1990s under very pessimistic assumptions.

We continued to meet, first at Baker's house (where we took time out from weekend negotiations to watch a Redskins football game together) and then at Blair House, the presidential guest house (actually a complex of town houses), from which Baker could walk across Pennsylvania Avenue to consult with Reagan. (Blair House also had the advantage of being just around the corner from the commission's headquarters at 736 Jackson Place.) Although we wanted to solve the long-run financing challenge — that is, to come up with enough money to cover outlays over the traditional 75-year estimating period — we naturally focused most of our attention on the short-run problem, because we had to be able to assure the principals that we could get the program to the 1990s.

The effect of the changes that we ended up advocating for the short run was to solve about two-thirds of the long-run problem. We had very different ideas about how to close the remaining gap. Within both our nine-person subgroup and the commission as a whole, the basic Republican position was to recommend raising the normal retirement age from 65 to 67 or 68. Those of us who had been appointed by Democrats were opposed to that, for the reasons that I had described to Darman. Moreover, we kept pointing out that a 75-year forecast is subject to many unforeseeable variables, and we said, in effect, "We're not sure that, after adopting the recommendations we can all agree to, there will actually be a long-run shortfall. But if one does develop, we would favor providing for an increase in the tax rates when needed rather than any cut in benefits." We thought our approach was superior, but it became clear that we would not be able to reconcile these opposite approaches to the remaining long-term deficit, and we didn't really try.

We did agree, however, that there was no need to be as pessimistic about the long run as I had been determined to be about the short run. As I've noted, I wanted us to rely on very pessimistic estimates for the short run because we needed to be absolutely sure that our proposals would take us to the 1990s — when, as we all agreed, the program would be in good shape for the next two decades or so. Greenspan and the White House negotiators were as anxious as I was to be sure that whatever we came up with would not prove to be a false promise. But for the long run there was no reason to choose such extremely pessimistic assumptions, and everyone agreed to stick with the middle-range estimates of Social Security's trustees — the estimates that had been used by successive administrations to assess the state of financing of the program. We were later accused of cherrypicking our assumptions to suit our purposes — that is, of trying to make the long-range picture look better than it really was — but that was definitely not the case.

Ideas in the night

A major remaining barrier to agreement involved the issue of moving up the scheduled payroll-tax increases. Within the negotiating group we were close to agreement on the desirability of moving the rate increase scheduled for 1990 to 1985. It was an essential step, but I knew that we would run into opposition when we took it to the entire commission for approval. Lane Kirkland had insisted all along that any acceleration of scheduled rate increases would have to be accompanied by refundable tax credits for workers. But the conservatives — particularly Bob Beck — saw that as a thinly veiled way to help finance Social Security from general revenues, and moreover as a potentially precedent-setting departure from the traditional 50-50 payroll tax split between employers and employees.

There seemed to be no way to resolve this conflict of wills. Then, just a day or two before the commission's new expiration date, I had a middle-of-the-night inspiration. My idea was to move the contribution rate increase scheduled for 1985 to 1984 — an increase not in our original plan — and to provide a refundable tax credit for that one year only.

Moving the 1985 rate to 1984 would get us sufficient additional income to finance the program through 1987. Since there would be no other tax increase over present law until 1988, there would be no need to decide until then whether to have another tax credit. I called Darman and Stockman, who agreed that this would be a breakthrough. I then queried Kirkland, who thought about it and concluded that getting a tax credit for one year would give him a precedent that he could use to argue for its extension later on. Beck, after considerable argument, managed to arrive at precisely the opposite conclusion — that enacting a tax credit for one year would *not* be precedent-setting and could be justified as easing the transition to higher tax rates for employees. So the idea worked. After the fact it seemed obvious.

Then, just as I was beginning to think that we might actually be within sight of an agreement, I learned that Baker, Darman, Greenspan, Dole, and Conable had something of a revolt on their hands. First, Armstrong had insisted on participating in the negotiations. That was his right, of course, as a member of the commission, but he was doggedly opposed to achieving any kind of balanced agreement — since he was interested only in blocking any tax increases and shriveling Social Security — and so he had nothing constructive to contribute. (He was not uncivil, however. At one point, during a break in the negotiations, he turned to me and said, "I'm opposed to everything you're doing, but I greatly admire the way you're doing it.")

Armstrong said hardly a word during any of the negotiating sessions he attended. He just listened and then communicated his concerns to the other conservatives on the commission. Apparently at his urging, several of the others — including Beck, Fuller, and Trowbridge — flew to Washington and insisted on meeting with Greenspan and Myers, to object to what was going on. They all felt that the agreement-in-progress relied too much on tax increases, and they wanted instead to slow the growth of program costs, partly by raising the retirement age and changing the benefit formula so that if the trust fund ratio (that is, the ratio of accumulated funds to the next year's outgo) fell below 20 percent, COLAs would be reduced by being based on the lesser of wage or price increases.

Beck was clearly the leader of the business group within the commission, and if he had refused to support a final agreement, Fuller and Trowbridge would have followed suit. Since Armstrong, Archer, and Waggonner were also opposed, the result would have been that only five Democrats and four Republicans on the commission would have supported the agreement — and Reagan would never have signed off on it.

My understanding is that Baker shepherded the dissidents one by one to the White House for quiet discussions with him and Dole, and that when Beck continued to be intractable, Baker ushered him into the Oval Office for a little chat with Reagan himself. Whatever the president said, it worked: Beck, Fuller, and Trowbridge fell into line, leaving only Archer, Armstrong, and Waggonner still opposed to a balanced agreement.

By January 14 we seemed very close to having that kind of agreement. The major sticking point on our side was the COLA delay. Baker and Darman were pressing for a six-month delay. I was reluctant to go that far without getting Claude Pepper's approval, since the whole idea of a COLA delay had been very hard for him to accept, and after his recent triumphs on the campaign trail he was only about half persuaded of the need to make concessions of *any* kind. But it was Friday afternoon, it had been a long week, we had made much progress and we were just a few hours away from the commission's final deadline — and Jim Baker was not much inclined to twiddle his thumbs while I tracked down Pepper and conferred with him. Baker was, as always, calm and courteous, but he told me, in effect, "I'm ready to take this entire package across the street to the President right now, and I believe he's ready to approve it."

After so many months of uncertainty (at best), he had my full attention as he dangled the prospect of immediate presidential approval before my eyes, all but promising that with just this one change we could have the agreement that I wanted so very much. I still needed to talk to Pepper, but I must say that at that moment Jim Baker's reputation as an astute negotiator was secure with me — long before I watched him represent George W. Bush so capably in the contested presidential election of 2000.

Our negotiating group met for the last time on the morning of Saturday, January 15, at Blair House, and agreed on a bipartisan solution that each side was willing to submit to its principals and then — if the principals accepted it — to the other members of the commission. The key points on which we had finally been able to agree were as follows (the short-term savings are shown in parentheses):

- *Moving up the scheduled tax rate increases:* The payroll tax increase scheduled for 1985 would be moved up to 1984, and the increase scheduled for 1990 to 1988, thus providing additional income for the trust fund, but with the initial tax increase for workers offset by a refundable tax credit ($40 billion).

- *Delaying the COLA:* Payment of the cost of living adjustment would be delayed for six months, with the result that in the future automatic increases would be made in the month of December rather than June ($40 billion).

- *Taxing benefits:* For higher-income beneficiaries, one-half of the Social Security benefit would henceforth be included in gross income for income tax purposes ($30 billion).

- *Covering more workers:* Social Security coverage would be extended to all federal employees newly hired after 1983, and to all employees of nonprofit organizations ($20 billion).

- *Increasing the contribution rate for the self-employed:* The rate for self-employed workers would be increased to two times the employee rate, but with one-half of the total contribution deductible as a business expense ($18 billion).

- *Making accounting changes:* The trust fund would be credited for payments owed by the federal government in connection with Social Security coverage provided during military service, and for uncashed benefit checks ($18 billion).

These six changes would result in short-term savings of $166 billion, and other, less significant changes would bring the total to $168 billion — enough to get Social Security to the "safe haven" of the 1990s. Although, as I've noted, our focus was always on the short term, these changes would also close most of the anticipated long-term deficit of 1.8 percent of payroll.

We also included a recommendation for a "stabilizer" — a provision to go into effect in 1988 as a way of guarding against the risk of the program once again running out of funds. If, at the beginning of a year, the money on hand in the trust fund was less than 20 percent of the projected outgo, the automatic cost-of-living adjustments would be based on whichever was lower: the increase in the Consumer Price Index or the increase in wages. (Among other things, this was a way of accommodating the Republicans on the commission who had sought this change.) And we recommended that the credit for delaying retirement should be increased from 3 percent per year to 8 percent, with the change to be phased in from 1990 to 2010. (This is happening as I write, and when the 8 percent level is reached in 2010, age 70 will be the age at which maximum benefits will be payable. Benefits applied for before age 70 will be actuarially reduced year-by-year down to age 62, the age of first eligibility for benefits.)

I felt very proud of what we had accomplished. We broke up at around noon, and most of the others left Blair House, letting the waiting reporters know that we would be reconvening later that afternoon. (Officially, the others all had work to catch up on. Most of them, however, actually spent the afternoon, as did the reporters, watching the Redskins play the

Minnesota Vikings in the National Football League playoffs.) I stayed behind to make some last-minute phone calls.

My first task was to check with Kirkland and Pepper. I knew from prior discussions that everything we had agreed to was acceptable to Moynihan and Keys, but I wasn't entirely sure about the others. The key point to confirm with Lane was that he could accept a payroll tax increase that had a refundable tax credit for 1984 only. The key point to confirm with Claude was that he could accept delaying the COLA by six months and putting it on a calendar-year basis for the future.

I decided that I'd better get Kirkland's approval first, so that I could tell Pepper that everyone else was on board. First I called O'Neill's people, bringing them up to date and telling them that I hoped to have everything wrapped up in an hour or so. It didn't quite work out that way.

I knew Kirkland was at the Drake Hotel in New York, but when I called him there I learned that he had just left and was on his way to board a train back to Washington. There were no cellphones in those days, of course, so it was quite late in the after noon before I was able to reach him, after he had finally arrived at his apartment. After I explained the entire package to him, he assured me that he could live with the one-year refundable tax credit and that if Pepper could accept the six-month COLA delay we should take the whole deal.

I reached Pepper in his apartment at around 5:00 P.M. He got his senior aide, Richard Lehrman, on the phone with us. After quite a bit of back and forth, he asked Richard what he thought, and Richard said he thought we had negotiated a good deal and should take it. Pepper said he agreed. I was now ready to see if the other side had gotten Reagan's endorsement. First, however, I called O'Neill's people again, to let them know that Kirkland and Pepper were aboard. As it happened, O'Neill and Rostenkowski were both in California, playing at the Bob Hope Desert Classic golf tournament in Palm Springs. We reached them at their hotel, where they were watching the Redskins on television, and so it was that the final proposal was simultaneously cleared with both the speaker of the House and the chairman of the Ways and Means Committee.

Then, just as everything seemed to be going really well (along with everything else, the Redskins had defeated the Vikings), we found ourselves in a last-minute hassle about how to announce the agreement. To my surprise, Baker and Darman suddenly sent word that Reagan and O'Neill would have to issue a joint announcement with exactly the same wording — or the whole deal was off.

They were adamant and surprisingly agitated. I suppose that even at this late hour Reagan was fearful that if he went first, and gave the agreement his ringing endorsement, O'Neill might then say something less fully supportive, making the president the fall guy for any criticism.

(To say that the two principals profoundly distrusted each other is a huge understatement. Reporters and historians have made much of their ability to banter together in public, but I know that in private Tip O'Neill detested Reagan. He told me on more than one occasion, with no attempt to mask his contempt, that the rich movie-actor president had long since forgotten his modest roots and had no sympathy for "the have-nots of America," as O'Neill put it. O'Neill, on the other hand, had never forgotten his own working-class upbringing. He revered Franklin D. Roosevelt, for whom he had campaigned door-to-door in 1932 as a 19-year-old political neophyte, and he considered it a very nearly sacred calling to preserve the heart and soul of FDR's legacy by saving Social Security.)

The White House had drafted a joint statement that seemed — to me — entirely acceptable. But O'Neill was having none of it. When we reached him at the room that he and Rostenkowski were sharing, Duberstein read the statement over the phone to Rostenkowski, who said he thought it was fine and asked O'Neill for his approval. "Not in my lifetime," O'Neill said. "There's not going to be any joint statement." He expanded on the point, in unprintable language. He then had his chief counsel, Kirk O'Donnell, draft a statement, and had it sent over to the White House. "Tell him to take it or leave it," O'Neill said. Fortunately Reagan opted to take it, and so it came to pass that Ronald Reagan and Tip O'Neill — two men who were unable to agree even on *how* to agree — ended up issuing separate statements proclaiming their equal support for the compromise solution we had worked out.

I explained all this to Moynihan when he returned to Blair House at around 6:00 P.M. By that time several other commission members had drifted in, and Pepper arrived soon afterward. Baker, Darman, Stockman, and Duberstein came over from the White House at around 7:00 P.M. with the good news that they were ready if we were. And so, with the principals on board, we went around the corner to the commission's headquarters on Jackson Place, where the remaining members of the commission were waiting, along with Bob Myers and Jack Svahn, the commissioner of Social Security.

Alan Greenspan explained the agreement and asked for a vote. It was, as we expected, 12–3, with Archer, Armstrong, and Waggonner opposed. Baker, Greenspan, and I ran upstairs to phone the president and let him know that we had an agreement. When we went back downstairs we found Claude Pepper holding forth at the center of a scrum of photographers and reporters, with a cluster of microphones in front of him and flashbulbs popping all around like a scene from a Frank Capra movie. The rest of us dutifully flanked him for a group photograph (in which we look rather anxious, probably because we had no idea what Pepper might say next). Then, after congratulating ourselves on what we had accomplished, we broke up at around midnight, walking out into Lafayette Park and the sight of the White House in fresh snow — a lovely scene, even to someone in a state of near-exhaustion.

Claude Pepper speaks to reporters. Listening are Bob Ball, Alan Greenspan, Pat Moynihan, Bill Armstrong, Mary Falvey Fuller, Barber Conable, and Bob Myers.

An ambitious legislative timetable

Our euphoria was short-lived. We still had to get our recommendations enacted as amendments to the Social Security Act. The legislative
process was to begin in just two weeks with a House Ways and Means
Committee hearing on February 1, and there was a pressing need to have
a law on the books by June. Otherwise Social Security would have insufficient funds on July 3 to send out, on time, the monthly benefit checks
owed to the more than 36 million men and women who were counting
on receiving them.

Hardly anyone wanted to see that happen. With opinion polls report-
ing 75 percent of the public disapproving of President Reagan's handling of
Social Security thus far, the White House was determined to get legislation
enacted as quickly as possible. So were Tip O'Neill, Dan Rostenkowski,
and most if not all of the other Democratic leaders, who saw nothing to
be gained — and much that would be put at risk — by delay.

The ball was now in Rostenkowski's court, since the House was con-
stitutionally responsible for initiating revenue legislation and the Ways
and Means Committee was the vehicle for that. Rostenkowski pledged
to complete committee hearings, mark up a bill, and get it to the floor
of the House for a vote by early March. Then if Bob Dole, chairing the
Senate Finance Committee, was able to set a similar speed record on his
side of the Capitol (where the bill to carry out the commission's recommendations received the designation S.1, emphasizing its priority status),
a House-Senate conference by mid-March might be possible, in which
case final enactment might be feasible before Congress adjourned for the
Easter recess on March 25. For anyone familiar with the normal pace of
Congress, this was obviously a very ambitious schedule.

Although just about everyone on Capitol Hill paid lip service to the
idea of fast-tracking the legislation — no one, after all, wanted to become
the target of 36 million outraged phone calls, telegrams, and letters — it
was by no means clear that the recommendations endorsed by Reagan
and O'Neill and adopted by the commission would survive the legislative process unscathed. Two of the three diehard critics within the
commission — Armstrong and Archer — were ready to fight for changes
that would have skewed the outcome to rely much more on benefit cuts
than on tax increases. Armstrong sat on the Senate Finance Committee;

Archer served on Ways and Means. They thus had platforms from which
to promote changes that, if adopted, could have undermined all the work
we had done.

Bob Dole outranked Armstrong and was confident of out-thinking him
as well, and Barber Conable as the senior Republican on Ways and Means
outranked Archer, but the two critics were still able to use their positions
to reinforce lobbyists' opposition and roil the legislative process. (During
the mark-up, for example, Archer introduced no less than 15 amendments,
all of which had to be discussed and voted on; in due course, with tempers
fraying, all of them were voted down.) And Armstrong and Archer had
some influential allies, including the other right-wingers in Congress and
some very vocal lobbyists.

Alan Greenspan and I were determined to present and maintain a
united front, and we did. When we briefed reporters immediately after the
commission's adoption of our package of recommendations on January 15,
we stressed the importance of keeping the package intact. As Greenspan
said: "The proposal is not in legislative language, and obviously it will be
changed in some respects. But the elements that make it up were very
tightly negotiated, and it was accepted as a total package. If you take a
significant portion out of the package, you will lose part of the consensus,
and the whole agreement will start to unravel."

We reinforced this message at every opportunity, and particularly
when we testified together before the Ways and Means Committee. We
agreed ahead of time that we would each testify in support of the entire
package, just as it was, including the parts that we personally had not
favored, and that I would respond to questions from the Democrats and
he would respond to the Republicans. Meanwhile, in the days just prior to
the hearings, I made countless phone calls and arranged many meetings
in an effort to ensure that the commission's recommendations would have
broad support among congressional leaders. Of particular importance
was a meeting I had with Senator Kennedy, the leader of the liberal bloc
in the Senate, at which I asked him to co-sponsor Dole's bill. At first he
was reluctant, thinking that he might be able to improve the outcome by
holding out. I suggested that doing so might well lead to the defeat of the
whole package. He then agreed to join forces with Dole, and soon sent
word that "everybody to Bob's left" would support his bill.

In the House the situation was somewhat more problematic — in part because, in solving only about two-thirds of the long-term deficit problem (since our primary focus was on getting Social Security safely to the 1990s), we had left the door open for proposals to close the remaining gap, regardless of whether such proposals had merit. As I've noted, the commission members appointed by Democrats were not convinced that a long-term shortfall would actually develop, and if it did, a tax increase could be provided for, to be implemented if needed. But the uncertainty about long-term forecasts provided an opening for those who, for various reasons, wanted to raise the retirement age or make other changes — such as changing the COLA formula — that would close the gap by reducing benefits. Jake Pickle, the conservative Texas Democrat who chaired the Social Security subcommittee of Ways and Means, was particularly determined to force through an increase in the normal retirement age as a way of slowing the growth of future outlays, and with hindsight it seems clear that neither Tip O'Neill nor I devoted enough energy to outmaneuvering him. (That said, I question whether it would have been possible, given the support that Pickle was able to pick up on both sides of the aisle.)

Greenspan and I did our best, however, to persuade Ways and Means members of the importance of preserving the package endorsed by the commission, and in my testimony I also stressed what I still consider to be one of the most important objectives — if not *the* most important — that I was able to achieve in our negotiations. That was the unanimous adoption by the commission of its number-one recommendation, really a statement of principle, which I had drafted:

> The members of the National Commission believe that the Congress, in its deliberations on financing proposals, should not alter the fundamental structure of the Social Security program or undermine its fundamental principles. The National Commission considered, but rejected, proposals to make the Social Security program a voluntary one, or to transform it into a program under which benefits are a product exclusively of the contributions paid, or to convert it into a fully-funded program, or to change it to a program under which benefits are conditioned on the showing of financial need.

I was pleased that the *New York Times,* in its analysis of the commission's recommendations, had picked up on this statement, emphasizing that the commission, despite the various changes it proposed, was calling for no major modifications to the fundamental commitment that Social Security represents. "That assurance," the *Times* stated, "already has emerged as the most enduring element of the proposal."

Outmaneuvering the lobbyists

Despite the commission's strong statement of principle and the broad support for its specific recommendations among congressional leaders and in the White House, there was intense opposition in some quarters.

For example, the federal employee unions adamantly opposed the commission's recommendation that new federal employees should be covered by Social Security, and they mounted a fierce lobbying campaign that nearly cost us the whole agreement. If we had lost that provision we theoretically might have been able to find another $20 billion somewhere to help get Social Security to the 1990s, but we had long since explored all the other revenue options and would almost certainly have had to accept more benefit cuts. Moreover, the lobbying campaign was designed to defeat the agreement at a point in the legislative process where, if the campaign had succeeded, there would have been little if any possibility of getting a bill passed by June 1983.

The federal employee unions really concerned themselves only with the interests of people who stay — or expect to stay — in government employment throughout their working lives. The unions didn't pretend to represent the interests of the large numbers of people who go in and out of government employment, for whom this provision would clearly be beneficial. Instead they told their lifelong-government-career members that the change would make it harder to retain or improve the civil service retirement system, which would become a supplement to Social Security. "You'll lose your bargaining power," the union leaders told their members — I assume sincerely — and their members believed it. They besieged their representatives in Congress, focusing mainly on the Senate, and were so effective that several Democratic senators withdrew their support for the change.

Toward the very end of the legislative process, when the House and Senate conferees had met and the House had accepted their report and passed a bill, the lobbying campaign became so intense that the Senate came very close to voting the bill down. Bob Dole called me from the

Senate floor, where he was managing the legislation and getting ready
to call for a vote, and told me that support was evaporating because of
the federal employees' opposition. He said, "This may wreck the whole
thing!" It was late in the evening, many senators had left the floor, and he
was nervous about bringing the bill to a vote. He asked me to phone some
Democratic senators who had spoken against the coverage provision to
see if they would come to the floor and reverse themselves in order to help
save the bill. I was able to reach Senator Don Riegle, and he tracked down
some of his colleagues, and they went to the Senate floor and voted for
the legislation. Unlike the federal employee unions, they weren't willing
to see the whole agreement wrecked over that one provision, which they
had been opposing only to placate the unions and not because they actually thought it would be harmful; they knew better. (And they were right:
federal employees today enjoy the additional protection of Social Security
without having lost their civil service retirement benefits.)

AARP, too, tried to block enactment of the legislation rather than acknowledging the need for compromise. They particularly stirred up their
members over the six-month delay in the COLA, which they correctly
saw as a permanent benefit cut but which in their lobbying they amplified
into a massive and unconscionable betrayal of the elderly. (In reality it
was a significant cut, although it doesn't sound significant, and a concession that I definitely did not like but that was absolutely necessary to get
an agreement.) Unable to generate sufficient support for eliminating the
provision in the Senate, they very nearly succeeded in the House by lobbying Claude Pepper and winning him over to their viewpoint — despite
his having approved the COLA delay in mid-January.

I knew nothing of Pepper's change of mind until I picked up the phone
one day, quite far along during the legislative process, and heard him
yelling at me. He told me he was in a meeting with AARP's lobbyists, and
he sounded very agitated. He said he hadn't understood that the six-month
COLA delay was going to affect benefits from then on out, as of course
was the case, and he accused me of deliberately misleading him. I tried
to respond, but he didn't want to listen. "The deal's off!" he shouted. "I'm
calling Greenspan, and then I'm calling the networks!"

I can't recall now whether I volunteered to go over to his office or
whether he demanded that I come over so that he could berate me in front

of the AARP people, but in any case I dropped whatever I was doing and headed over to his office. First, however, I spoke with Richard Lehrman, Pepper's chief staff person, who had closely monitored the commission's deliberations from beginning to end. I was sure that he fully understood the effect of the COLA delay. He confirmed that he did, and said he would try to persuade Pepper to hold off on calling Greenspan or anyone else until I got there.

I called Tip O'Neill's staff to warn them of this possible insurrection, and then on the way out the door I had an inspiration. I called Wilbur Cohen, explained the situation, and asked him to call Dick Bolling, who was Pepper's predecessor as chairman of the House Rules Committee. Bolling had recently retired from Congress, but he and Pepper were still very close. My thought was that Bolling should telephone Pepper and congratulate him on what a wonderful thing he had accomplished on the commission.

While I was in Pepper's office, the call from Bolling came through. Pepper was hard of hearing and always kept the volume on his phone turned up, so I could hear Dick telling him what a great package he had negotiated and that it was a masterful thing to have ended up with just a COLA delay rather than having to accept deeper benefit cuts as the price of getting an agreement with the White House. Claude was visibly pleased. "You really think so?" he kept asking. Bolling said he did, and added that he thought it was especially shrewd to have crafted the agreement in such a way that the whole thing would unravel if any of the recommendations were dropped. When Claude got off the phone he told the AARP people everything Bolling had said, stated that he fully understood the impact of the COLA delay and accepted it as the price of getting an agreement with the White House, thanked them courteously for their time and ushered them out the door.

To this day I'm not sure how much of his indignation was real and how much of it may have been just a show for the AARP people. It could have been some of both. Pepper was certainly capable of political grandstanding for influential constituents. But it may be that he really hadn't understood how delaying the COLA and shifting it to a calendar-year basis would constitute a permanent cut. (Indeed, in January he had told reporters: "We would be willing to consider one deferment of the cost-of-living adjustment, but as part of a package that would guarantee no cut in benefits.") As I sat with him it occurred to me that if in fact he was confused, he ought to be careful about revealing it. He was 82 years old, and his many critics were more than ready to paint him as a befuddled oldster who ought to relinquish his powerful committee chairmanship. He didn't need to hand them ammunition. Whatever the true story was, after the AARP people left he was all smiles. But I wasn't taking any chances. The last thing I needed was to have him change his mind again and go on television to claim he'd been snookered. So I stayed for a while, carefully going over each of the commission's recommendations and their consequences, until Richard Lehrman and I were both confident that Pepper was firmly on board.

Pepper was, of course, a critically important ally, both within the commission and then during the legislative process when the issue of how to close the remaining long-term shortfall had to be addressed. As I've noted, within the commission the five of us appointed by Democrats took the position that if a revenue shortfall did indeed develop at some point during the 75-year estimating period, it could be addressed by scheduling a contribution-rate increase to be put into effect only if needed. Most of the other members of the commission rejected that approach, preferring to raise the retirement age instead — a solution that Lane Kirkland in particular found offensive. "That may be fine for someone dreaming up policy options in a think tank," he would say. "For them it's inside work and no heavy lifting [as John F. Kennedy famously said of the presidency] and they don't care when they retire. But try telling a steel-mill worker or a coal miner or a factory hand to just work a few more years!"

The White House negotiators were no more sympathetic to our point of view than the Republicans on the commission had been. Their focus, of course, was on dealing with Social Security's immediate funding crisis and getting the program safely to the 1990s, and so the question of how to address the remaining long-term shortfall was still unresolved when we delivered our recommendations to Reagan and O'Neill in mid-January. It then became an issue for the Congress to take up.

Pepper was adamantly opposed to increasing the retirement age and championed the alternative approach of enacting a payroll tax increase in 2015 if needed to forestall a shortfall. Fresh from his successes on the campaign trail in 1982, he was confident that he could prevail in the House.

But Jake Pickle, who had long sought to enact a retirement age increase, only to be effectively muzzled by Tip O'Neill in 1981, was determined to get his way in 1983. He had many allies among conservative Democrats and — more importantly for the outcome — among Republicans as well. Some of them supported a retirement age increase on the merits (as they saw the merits), but others were still sore at Pepper for the way he had campaigned against them and for the seats he had cost them, and were just out for revenge.

"The battle of the condiments"

O'Neill was more focused on getting our recommendations enacted intact than on how best to address a hypothetical long-term shortfall, and Rostenkowski was focused on preserving his fast-track legislative timetable. At all costs he wanted to avoid — first in committee and then on the floor — a debate that he regarded as of secondary importance but that would consume precious time. And so Rostenkowski and O'Neill decided to streamline the process, ruling that Pickle and Pepper would each be given an opportunity to offer their proposals on the floor, but only in pure form — that is, without sweeteners to attract support — and the House would then have to vote each proposal up or down. Thus what more than one wag described as "the battle of the condiments" — Pickle vs. Pepper — moved to its denouement.

When the debate took place, early in March, Pickle spoke first. He had wanted to improve his odds by proposing only a one-year increase in the normal retirement age, from 65 to 66, but Social Security's actuaries had advised him that doing so would not slow the growth of outlays enough to close the potential shortfall. So he was stuck with going to 67, an increase that the AFL-CIO and others regarded as unwarranted. (I shared that assessment, in part because it amounted to a substantial benefit cut and because no one knew how such an increase, even if gradually put into effect as proposed, would affect individuals, the workforce, productivity, and the economy, and so I regarded the actuaries' estimates of its effect on the shortfall as quite conjectural.) Of course the AFL-CIO opposed *any* increase, even if gradually put into effect as Pickle proposed, and many Democratic members of the House were anxious about invoking the wrath of constituents nearing retirement. But on the day of the debate

Rostenkowski made it clear that he supported Pickle, and at that point few Democrats saw anything to be gained by crossing the powerful Ways and Means chairman. Pickle's amendment passed, 228–202.

Pepper was taken aback by the vote. He made an impassioned speech, arguing that the House in "twiddling" over ways to cut benefits was losing sight of what Social Security had accomplished in saving millions of people from poverty and misery and the loss of their dignity. Pepper was a masterful orator, and when he finished he received a standing ovation from his colleagues on both sides of the aisle. But when his amendment came up for a vote, it failed badly. The Democrats were split, and only one Republican voted in favor. The vote was 296–132.

With that kind of lopsided margin in favor of raising the retirement age over what I still regard as our much superior approach — a scheduled tax increase held in reserve to be used only if and when needed — it became clear that a retirement age increase would be adopted by both houses of Congress, and in due course it was. There were, I think, several reasons why that happened, including the fact that the AFL-CIO lobbyists were working so hard trying to prevent extension of coverage to federal employees that they let the retirement-age issue get away from them. And Tip O'Neill hadn't paid all that much attention to blocking it. I'm not sure how much he cared about it, but in any case he didn't put his back into defeating it. In the end, Claude Pepper tried to put a good face on his defeat. He would point out that the increase would not begin going into effect until 2000, and he would say, "We've got lots of time to fix that!" At 82, he knew quite well that he might not actually have lots of time, as indeed he did not,[6] but he was a paragon of optimism.

And on the issue at hand, he was right. I still see no merit in raising the retirement age. I see it as having the effect of an across-the-board benefit cut without any redeeming features. And I see it as discriminating against people who have spent their lives in physically demanding work and who really *need* to quit, and ought to be able to do so without seeing their benefits significantly reduced when they find it necessary to retire before reaching the age of eligibility for full benefits. I share Lane Kirkland's views on this. It has always troubled me to hear academic economists advocating

---

6 *Editor's note:* Claude Pepper died in 1989.

changes to Social Security that wouldn't hurt them at all, but that definitely *would* be harmful to someone who has been working on a Ford assembly line for decades and is hoping to have a few years to do something less demanding with the help of his or her Social Security benefits. As a result of the enactment of this change we now have a large socioeconomic experiment under way.[7] We have no idea what the results will be. We don't know if people will want to work longer, or whether their employers will want them to. We don't know how millions of people will be affected. Yet today we're hearing that the retirement age should be increased still further. My view is that there is nothing magical about 65, or 67 for that matter, and perhaps we can design an economic system that encourages everyone to work to 70 or even beyond — if that's what we all want — but I object to setting things up so that someone who really needs to retire earlier, for whatever reason, is forced to take a big reduction in benefits. And I would certainly wait to see how this first experiment turns out before I would even consider raising the retirement age any further.

But with that exception I remain generally well satisfied with the outcome of our last-minute negotiations and the legislative process that followed them. We rescued Social Security from the short-term crisis caused by the stagflation of the 1970s. We came up with the revenue needed to get the program safely to the 1990s and far beyond, without imposing any draconian benefit cuts. The recommendations that emerged from my negotiations with Jim Baker withstood attacks from many quarters and have withstood the test of time. The long-term shortfall that Social Security faces today is the subject for another chapter of this memoir, but suffice it to say that the shortfall — which I consider eminently manageable — arose largely because of changed actuarial assumptions about the future performance of the economy and not because of anything we did or failed to do in 1983.

---

7 *Editor's note:* The Social Security Amendments of 1983 gradually increase the normal retirement age — from 65 in 2000 to 67 in 2027. The Social Security Administration notes on its website: "The Congress cited improvements in the health of older people and increases in average life expectancy as primary reasons for increasing the normal retirement age." Whatever Congress may have cited, however, the real and primary reason for the increase was that this was a way to slow the growth of outlays, as indicated in the debate between Jake Pickle and Claude Pepper. The increase has the same effect as an across-the-board cut in benefits for workers born after 1935, and particularly for workers born after 1960.

The rescue legislation was signed into law on April 20, 1983, just four months before there would have been insufficient funds to pay full benefits on time. (The drop-dead date had receded slightly, from July to August.) At an elaborate ceremony on the south lawn of the White House, President Reagan delivered a ringing endorsement of the legislation:

> This bill demonstrates for all time our nation's ironclad endorsement of Social Security. It assures the elderly that America will always keep the promises it made in troubled times a half a century ago. It assures those who are still working that they, too, have a pact with the future. From this day forward, they have our pledge that they will get their fair share of benefits when they retire....
>
> A tumultuous debate about Social Security has raged for more than two decades in this country; but there has been one point that has won universal agreement. The Social Security system must be preserved.... Today we reaffirm Franklin Roosevelt's commitment that Social Security

President Reagan signs the Social Security Amendments of 1983 into law. Watching are Bob Dole, Jake Pickle, Claude Pepper, House Minority Leader Bob Michel, Pat Moynihan, Tip O'Neill, Barber Conable, and Howard Baker (with camera).

must always provide a secure and stable base so that older Americans may live in dignity.

Sitting on the platform near the president, I listened to his words and thought that it was a wonderful statement, especially coming from a man who had long wanted to make Social Security voluntary — knowing, as of course he must have, that to do so would have undermined rather than affirmed Franklin Roosevelt's commitment. But even so — or perhaps especially in light of that historical fact — it was a fine statement, and the ceremony, with Tip O'Neill standing next to Reagan, was a great show of unity in support of Social Security.

Why did we succeed?

At the signing ceremony, Jim Baker introduced me to his son as "the man who solved the problem." I would say much the same of him. In our negotiations he was able to put ideology aside and focus on the substance of what had to be done to get an agreement that would meet the needs of both sides. He was also very clearly in charge on his side of the table. I was not at all surprised when, 17 years later, he was able to serve George W. Bush so skillfully in resolving the disputed presidential election of 2000, or that he later co-chaired the commission that tried to find a way out of the Iraq war. Unfortunately, even after that experience he still seems to think that bipartisan commissions are a good way to tackle difficult subjects.

Soon after his memoir was published, I wrote to him to correct his description of the Greenspan Commission as "a great success [that] worked out a genuine compromise between those who wanted to increase taxes and those who wanted to reduce benefits." I reminded him that the Greenspan Commission as such had failed to reach consensus, that the negotiations to which he referred had taken place only after the commission had failed, and that it was only after getting the blessing of the two principals, Reagan and O'Neill, that we secured the formal backing of the commission — a total reversal of the usual process for advisory groups.

He wrote back on January 5, 2007, acknowledging that I was "absolutely right" in my recollection of the facts but then adding:

> I do, however, continue to believe that what we were able to accomplish should become a model for dealing with Social Security because, in my

view, it is only when we take this issue "out of politics" through a negotiation involving the leadership of both parties that we can be successful. I also continue to believe that what we were able to accomplish was
of substantial benefit to our country and trust that you feel likewise. It
would never have happened without your participation for two reasons:
first, your expertise with the subject and second, Tip O'Neill's total
confidence in you.

I replied, thanking him and assuring him that I too was pleased with
the result. But I wanted to get across an important point:

> As of course you know, the commission became primarily a cover for
> the negotiations between the leaders of the two parties, Reagan and
> O'Neill. I agree that this is the only approach that would have worked
> in 1983. I don't believe, however, that the time is right for the leaders of
> the two parties to negotiate a new [Social Security] agreement. With
> private defined-benefit pension plans covering only about 20 percent of
> the private labor force and with the percentage declining (401(k) plans
> are an inadequate substitute), and with private savings having dropped
> last year to a negative rate, I don't believe Democrats should agree to
> any Social Security benefit cuts. What is there for them to negotiate
> when after 2008 there might be a president who would agree that cuts
> are neither necessary nor desirable?

In short, I worry greatly when I hear the Greenspan Commission
being touted as a model for negotiations over the future of Social Security. I am afraid that it would become, instead, a mechanism to generate
support for compromises that Democrats should feel no need or inclina-
tion to accept.

I received many congratulatory letters and phone calls after the signing
ceremony. Two in particular stand out in memory. One was a call from
Bob Dole, asking if I would work with him to solve Medicare's financial
shortfall. After thinking it over, I regretfully declined his offer. I felt that
there was not enough possibility of reaching an agreement on that subject
to make for a successful negotiating partnership. But it says much about
Bob Dole — and the mutual trust that we developed after working together
to rescue Social Security — that he made the offer.

The second call came from President Reagan. As I recall, he was at
Camp David, where communications were handled by the military. Doris

answered the phone, and the voice on the other end said, "This is Sergeant So-and-So. The President wants to talk to Mr. Ball. Is he there?" Doris snapped to attention and said, "Yes, *sir!*" As Doris was handing me the phone, I whispered, "You don't have to salute!"

The president was very warm and gracious. He gave me a lot of credit for working things out. "I called to thank you and salute you," he said. I reciprocated by assuring him that his staff had been top-notch negotiating partners. And indeed that was the case.

Which brings me to the final points I want to make about the National Commission on Social Security Reform and the key factors that account for the success of the extraordinary negotiations of January 1983:

- Alan Greenspan's low-key, completely fair handling of his chairmanship set a tone that helped make civilized discussions possible, particularly after he and I agreed to avoid all statements of philosophical positions during the early consideration of issues. Similarly, his willingness to develop a list of possible changes and our being able to agree on their financial impact helped lay the groundwork for everything that followed, including the January 1983 negotiations.

- The fact that the system was about to run short of enough money to pay full benefits on time concentrated the attention of the commissioners — albeit not enough. It *definitely* concentrated the attention of the January 1983 negotiators. Anything less than that level of urgency might not have produced an agreement.

- The final negotiations were greatly facilitated by being conducted entirely by members of the commission and top members of the White House staff. We did not need to turn to subordinate staff for guidance, nor did we have to deal with any agendas that anyone else might have brought to the table.

- The key people in the final negotiations fortunately were the least ideological and most flexible of all the people involved since the inception of the commission. Pragmatism was an absolutely essential precondition for arriving at an agreement.

- Allowing the principals to stay one step removed while we negotiated by proxy was also essential for success. Reagan and O'Neill were always up to date but never until the last day of negotiations had to commit themselves, thereby avoiding getting locked into any public positions that could have led to deadlock.

▪ Nothing, however, should obscure the fact that the National Commission on Social Security Reform was *not* an example of a successful bipartisan commission. The commission itself stalled — essentially deadlocked, despite continuing to talk — after reaching agreement on the size of the problem that needed to be addressed. As a commission, that was as far as it got. The usual commission procedure was then turned on its head. An agreement was negotiated between the principals by proxy and then the already agreed-to result was taken back to the commission for its endorsement.

▪ Whether such an inversion could work in the future is arguable — depending, as it would, on specific circumstances as well as on the personalities of the principals and their proxies — but to suggest that the Greenspan Commission provides a model for resolving questions about Social Security's future would be laughable if it were not so dangerous. Democrats in Congress who believe in strengthening rather than undermining Social Security should be willing to stand up for what they believe — preferably with a strong supporter of Social Security in the White House—but stand up in any case. A commission is no substitute for principled commitment. Above all, we should not allow ourselves to fall into the trap of expecting miracles from another Greenspan Commission — by deluding ourselves into believing, mistakenly, that the first one was a great success.

"A commission is no substitute for principled commitment."

To Bob Ball –
With appreciation and thanks
for a job well done on the solving
of the Social Security Program –
You are a just American –
Tip O'Neill
Speaker

Index